CRIMINAL CRAFTS

Outlaw Projects for Scoundrels, Cheats, and Armchair Detectives

Shawn Gascoyne-Bowman

Photographs by Laura Sams and Robert Sams

Andrews McMeel Publishing, LLC

Kansas City · Sydney · London

Andrews McMeel Publishing, LLC
an Andrews McMeel Universal company
1130 Walnut Street, Kansas City, Missouri 64106

www.andrewsmcmeel.com

12 13 14 15 16 WKT 10 9 8 7 6 5 4 3 2 1

ISBN: 978-1-4494-0985-2

Library of Congress Control Number: 2011932638

Book design by Holly Ogden
Photography by Laura Sams and Robert Sams, www.sisbro.com
Additional art by Giuseppe Lipari, www.studiolipari.com

www.criminalcrafts.com

Attention: Schools and Businesses

Andrews McMeel books are available at quantity discounts with bulk purchase for educational, business, or sales promotional use. For information, please e-mail the Andrews McMeel Publishing Special Sales Department:
specialsales@amuniversal.com

CONTENTS

Recipes for Disaster
50 WAYS TO CLEAVE YOUR LEAVER 79

Home Is Where the Heart Is . . . and the Left Leg, and the Spleen
DECOR FOR YOUR DEN OF THIEVES 105

Thank-Yous

Putting together a book is a lot like pulling off a big heist: It takes years of planning and a tight crew of geniuses. My heartfelt thanks go out to: Xander, my demolitions expert; Lucy the puppet master; Bo, my partner in crime and manager of offshore accounts; Sorche, who's got my probation officer on speed dial; Lane Butler, funky font master Holly Ogden, and the outstanding crew at Andrews McMeel; Popeye, my consigliere; Bobby Tom, for maintaining my fleet of getaway vehicles; San Antonio Pat, the titular head of our crime family; "Auntie" Linda, my bookie; Pooch, for making me look pretty; Ms. Dawkins of the Tragically Charming Living Room; the handsome David Walker, a.k.a. Dr. No Love; V-town Julie, for minding my p's and q's; and, of course, Amy, my nemesis.

I'm especially lucky to have collaborated with the amazingly talented brother-and-sister team of Laura Sams and Robert Sams—ex-pirates, filmmakers, and occasionally shark bait. Their expertise in photography, computers, and taxidermy proved invaluable.

Thanks also go to Sckavone's, Rocking Frog Café, the Someday Lounge, and the Oregon Film Museum in Astoria for letting us come in and take pictures. The Portland Police Museum is inspirational and a great place for doing research; it's nice to be on the other side of the bars for a change. Friends of Tryon Creek State Park and Paxton Gate, Portland, assisted enormously in the loan of stuffed squirrels "Stumpy" and "Stumpy Two," respectively. If you ever find yourself in the Pacific Northwest, it would be a crime to miss these fine establishments.

Introduction to the Dark Arts

It isn't often in life that we are afforded the opportunity to mix business with pleasure. Ironically, this thought struck me during my last little visit to the big house. After a couple of minor indiscretions, I was forced to cool my heels for a few months—but on the upside I could network with associates, and hopefully pick up a new skill, like knitting on a shoestring, or in my case, knitting *with* a shoestring because my yarn stash was declared contraband.

During this imposed "vacation" I realized criminals and crafters truly have lots in common: time on their hands, sticky fingers that can't stay still, and a knack for repurposing anything that isn't bolted down into either a tool for busting out or an objet d'art.

Little-known fact:

The term *shabby chic* actually originated at Folsom Prison.

When the full oeuvre of criminal and crafting hobbies is considered, from self-inflicted tattoos to poodle-shaped Kleenex cozies made from pom-poms, a common thread unwinds—these folks are pathological makers. The world is their canvas to embellish, tweak, glitter, and occasionally set on fire.

The pinstripe cloth cuts both ways. Consider two of the twentieth century's more notorious icons: John Dillinger and Martha Stewart. Dillinger, Public Enemy No. 1, purportedly fashioned a mock gun out of a bar of soap and shoe polish, using it to escape from the Crown Point, Indiana, county jail. Brilliant! With limited resources he created a functional object (which doubled as a great gift), and was able to make a clean getaway.

On the flip side of the paint chip we have Martha Stewart, America's Patron Saint of Craft. The woman who sleeps with a glue gun under her pillow was convicted of no less than four felony charges, including conspiracy to obstruct justice, perjury, making false statements to federal prosecutors (two counts), and obstruction of justice. Personally, I think Martha got a bum rap on that one, but I'm biased. She once gave me a cookie (just before having me removed from her set), and while I might hold a grudge, I'm no cookie hater.

Although the lines between scrapbookers and convicts can get somewhat blurry, they positively disintegrate when you throw a little espionage into the mix. Where would a successful spy be without hollow books, see-behind sunglasses, and homemade instant disguises?

Perusing the lineup of usual DIY suspects, let's not forget the noir femme fatale. This pulp fiction trollop might be better known for leading good men astray rather than for her domestic skills, but believe me, those little vixens are house-proud, and handy at a bit more than laundering the money and cooking the books. Who better than a curvy strumpet to deliver a cake with a file inside or knockout cocktail recipes— make mine a Double Agent!

From sprucing up your cell to concocting a recipe for disaster, *Criminal Crafts* has a little something for everyone. The projects featured in this book won't cost you an arm and a leg, either (maybe a pinkie, but that's if you don't pay up in time). Heaven knows, it's hard to be a gangster, and spending money to make money never made much sense to me. Whenever possible, featured crafts utilize materials you probably already have sitting around the house: duct tape, a hammer, Pop Rocks, lock-picking tools . . . So, bust out your inner felon—it's time to get crafty.

CRIMINAL INTENT

practical Projects for Getting the Job Done

RANSOM NOTE KIT

Have you ever found yourself in the midst of creating a "love letter, straight from your heart," when you realized the recycling went out yesterday and the only newspaper lying about the house is a slightly incriminating back issue of *Pravda*? You've dug through the trash for twenty minutes and you just couldn't find a letter *J*, as in "just bring unmarked twenties."

The Ransom Note Kit features a decoy cigar box or heart-shaped candy box lined with small paper baking cups, one for each letter of the alphabet, with a larger compartment set aside for a glue stick, tweezers, and disposable gloves to conceal your ever-so-personal fingerprints. With this efficient system, magazines can swiftly be deconstructed and letters categorized, freeing up your valuable time for executing bigger things.

SUPPLIES

26 extra-small baking cup liners (see Note)

Cigar box or other gift box big enough to fit the liners and your tools

Craft glue or hot glue gun

Letters cut from magazines

Glue stick

Tweezers

Disposable gloves (optional)

HOW TO

1. Lay out the liners in the base of the box and decide your preferred arrangement. Make sure to leave room for your glue stick and tweezers. If your box is extra big you could also make a space for disposable gloves.

2. Glue the bottom of the cups to the inside bottom of the box.

3. Separate the cut letters alphabetically into the cups.

Note:
Paper candy cups are the perfect sized liner, leaving room inside your box for tools and gloves.

Some Tips for Manifestos and Other Rants

-- Cut larger letters from magazines-- ½- to 1-inch letters make a stunning visual impression.

-- Vary the look of your letters by mixing up fonts and colors. You'll probably need to skim through a variety of magazines to stock your supply.

-- Kids' and design magazines tend to have lots of interesting letters to choose from.

-- Steer clear of exotic and foreign periodicals if you are hoping to keep your identity secret; paperboys and mailmen tend to remember suspects with obscure interests.

-- Keep your message short and to the point.

-- Make sure to misspell at least one word. This gives the false impression of a lack of professionalism and thuggishness, plus it makes you sound scary.

Voodoo Doll Pincushion

Perhaps, like me, your dreams have been crushed. Someone you love has ripped out your heart and thrown it to the wolves, leaving you a burning desire to return the favor. A voodoo doll pincushion is a great way to exorcise a little angst while tidying up the sewing room, and it makes a fetching bracelet, too!

Ankle-deep in white chiffon, I was sewing my heart out when the phone rang: Gaston calling to say, "No, no. Not cold feet, my love, but perhaps we're rushing things a tad." A June wedding was not in my future. Through my tears, I could hardly find the seam ripper, much less the needle I'd set down a moment earlier. Why couldn't manipulating my Cajun cutie be as easy as crafting? Rather than fabricate an alibi, I decided to torture his effigy instead—one worn on my wrist, keeping him close at all times. I added a protective layer of plastic inside the cushion, fashioned from a recycled food container, to make sure my arm was well guarded from vigorous jabs of "He loves me, he loves me not, he loves me, loves me, loves ME!" Oh, Gaston, you will be mine.

SUPPLIES

- Heavyweight tracing paper
- Empty plastic salad container or other lid larger than 5 x 3 inches
- Scissors
- Straight pins
- 2 sheets craft felt in contrasting colors
- ½-inch-wide elastic, long enough to encircle wrist (about 9 to 12 inches)
- Fabric chalk
- Sewing needle and heavy-duty thread to match the elastic
- Craft glue
- Embroidery needle
- Embroidery floss in a contrasting color to your felt
- Cotton, polyfill, or your favorite stuffing

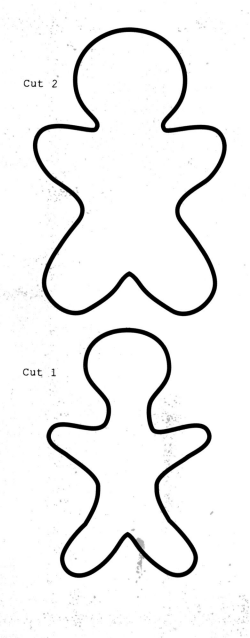

Cut 2

Cut 1

HOW TO

1. Copy the patterns and enlarge 166 percent.

2. Using the paper template, trace the smaller design onto the scrap plastic container--crafty criminals recycle! Cut out the shape.

3. Pin the larger outline to one of the sheets of felt and cut out two pieces, A and B.

4. Measure and cut the elastic to fit comfortably around your wrist with the ends slightly overlapping; mark the overlap with fabric chalk. Using

heavy-duty thread, sew several stitches to tack the elastic together at the chalk line, then sew around the overlap for reinforcement.

5. Stitch the wristband to one side of felt piece A at the elastic seam.

6. Glue the plastic doll shape to the side of felt piece A, opposite the elastic band. Aside from giving your cushion stability, the plastic ensures you won't be stabbing pins into your wrist during enthusiastic sewing/voodoo curse sessions.

7. From the contrasting colored felt, cut two small circles for eyes.

8. Using six strands of embroidery floss, sew the eyes to one side of felt piece B. Sew X shapes on the eyes if you want to give your dolls that creepy zombie look. Sew a free-form mouth.

9. Use a running stitch to sew felt pieces A and B together with wrong sides facing, leaving a leg open for inserting the stuffing.

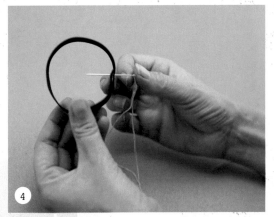

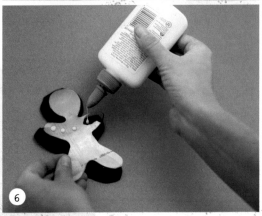

10. Stuff the doll with the polyfill and then finish sewing A and B together.

11. Place the doll on your wrist and admire it. Begin your next sewing project, or light candles for cursing incantations-- whatever your personal situation might dictate at the time . . .

John Dillinger Soap Gun

What have I told you about leaving fingerprints everywhere?

Go wash your hands! Nothing says "amateur criminal" like a messy crime scene.

This handmade cleansing bar is named after John Dillinger, the Depression-era bank robber who successfully escaped from the Crown Point, Indiana, county jail using a bar of soap he'd carved into the shape of a gun. While this craft can't make you a master criminal, it can promise you a clean getaway.

The refreshing scents of eucalyptus and mint help you fight Public Enemy No.1: bad body odor. With gorgeous pearl handle details and silky lather, this soap will look mighty sharp sitting in the guest lavatory.

Supplies for this craft are easily found online at soapmaking and baking supply sites.

SUPPLIES

1 pound clear melt-and-pour soap base (see Sources)

1 pound white melt-and-pour soap base

2 (8-cup) metal mixing bowls (not plastic, for Pete's sake)

Cooking pot that is slightly smaller than your metal mixing bowls

Pot holder

1 ounce soap fragrance oil (I like mint and eucalyptus; see Sources)

Metal whisk

Small ladle or gravy spoon

Plastic gun molds (see Note and Sources)

1 ounce black soap colorant (see Sources)

HOW TO

1. Dice the soap bases into large chunks and place each color in a separate metal mixing bowl.

2. Fill the small pot halfway with water, place it on the stove, and bring the water to a low boil.

3. Put the metal bowl with the white soap base over the boiling water. We're creating a double boiler here, where the heat is evenly distributed across the surface area of the mixing bowl and can be removed quickly if things get too hot. Have a pot holder ready--your bowl will heat up fast!

4. Add 3 to 5 drops of fragrance to the melting soap base and stir with a metal whisk.

5. Spoon or ladle the melted white soap into the handles of the gun molds. Let cool for several minutes. Use a small paring knife to trim away any soap that has spilled out of the handle area and return the scraps to the mixing bowl. Use a pot holder to remove the bowl from the pot and set it aside. If necessary, add more water to the pot and bring it back to a low boil.

6. To the clear soap base chunks, add 5 to 10 drops of black colorant and 3 to 5 drops of fragrance. Place the bowl over the boiling water and let melt, gently stirring until you have a consistent color of soap.

7. Spoon or ladle the melted soap into the remaining spaces of the gun molds until each is filled. Any excess black soap can be trimmed and thrown back into the bowl after the gun has cooled.

8. Let the soap cool for 30 minutes or more, then flip the molds upside down and pop the soaps out. Avoid the temptation to cool the soaps in the refrigerator or freezer, as this may cause them to "sweat" and get a fuzzy water-condensation coating. You may run into sweat issues, too, if you live somewhere humid. You could try a low/no-sweat brand of melt-and-pour soap base, or place the soaps in front of a fan after they have been removed from the mold.

9. Remelt the soap bases and repeat the process.

10. Now get out there and do something dirty. You've earned it, and for once you won't need a bagman to clean up afterward.

Note:

The supplies for this recipe make about a dozen 3-ounce soap guns. Your results may vary depending on what type of gun you are making and the size of your mold. The most common molds I've seen have either one or two pistols in them, so you'll be making two or three guns at a time and repeating the process after each set is cooled and popped out.

Día de los Muertos Bath Fizzies

My crafty shenanigans tend to land me in hot water, and after a long day's scheming and stalking, there is nowhere I'd rather be than that warm, fragrant tub. To best enjoy my repose and to match my macabre decor, I've constructed festive skull-shaped bath fizzies. They contain a refreshing skin softener, and best of all, small, devious treats can be hidden inside.

Traditional *calaveras* are made for the Mexican celebration Día de los Muertos, when deceased loved ones are honored and their spirits invited back to the family home to share a meal and a shot of tequila, and to party. The ornately decorated skulls are made from sugar and royal icing, with the name of the deceased often written on the forehead.

For my luxury soak, I've swapped out the sugar for a bath fizzy mix and used a *calavera* mold, which can be ordered online or found in specialty shops. With a few drops of fragrance oil, you'll be smelling just as sweet as the afterlife.

To spice up my skulls even further, I've hidden small toys such as SuperBalls and fake bugs inside. They magically appear as the fizzies dissolve in the bath.

SUPPLIES

SKULLS

Makes 8 medium (3-ounce) skulls

2 cups baking soda

1 cup citric acid (see Sources)

1 cup cornstarch

6 tablespoons jojoba oil

4 teaspoons witch hazel (see Note)

2 tablespoons water

10 drops fragrance oil

Calavera molds (see Sources)

Small toy (optional)

ICING

3/4 cup meringue powder

1 cup powdered sodium lauryl sulfate (see Sources)

1 cup confectioners' sugar (plus more if needed)

3/4 teaspoon cream of tartar

1/2 cup warm water

4 tablespoons jojoba oil

5 drops fragrance oil

A few drops of bath-safe colorant (see Sources)

TO MAKE THE SKULLS:

1. Sift the baking soda, citric acid, and cornstarch together into a large mixing bowl and stir with your hands, making sure to break up any hard-packed chunks.

2. In a separate bowl, whisk together the jojoba oil, witch hazel, water, and fragrance oil.

3. Add the wet ingredients to the dry a few tablespoons at a time, stirring thoroughly with your hands until the mixture has the consistency of wet sand.

4. The mix should hold a shape when squeezed together firmly. If it doesn't, add a bit more of the liquid ingredients, a few drops at a time.

5. Pack the mixture firmly into the molds.

6. Flip the molds upside down onto a clean, flat surface. The fizzy forms should tap out easily. If they don't, your mixture may be too wet. Toss any cracked or broken skulls back into the mixing bowl, add a pinch more cornstarch, and try again.

7. To hide a treat in each *calavera*, you'll need to line the bottom and sides of the mold with about ⅛ inch of the fizzy mixture. Put the small toy inside, then cover completely and pack firmly with fizzy mixture.

TO DECORATE:

1. To make the icing, combine the meringue mix, sodium lauryl sulfate, confectioners' sugar, and cream of tartar in a bowl.

2. In a separate bowl, mix together the water, jojoba oil, and fragrance oil.

3. Whisk the wet ingredients into the dry. Your icing should have the consistency of thick toothpaste. If it is too thin, you can add a bit more confectioners' sugar. If it is too thick, add a few drops of water.

4. Add the colorant last. I like to use lots of colors when decorating, and I usually divide my icing into three or four bowls at this point, adding a different color to each. While you are working, make sure to cover the icing you aren't using with plastic wrap so it doesn't dry out.

5. Put the icing into a pastry bag
   (or a resealable plastic bag
   with one corner snipped off) and
   pipe onto the skulls.

6. Sprinkle with decorative colored
   sugar for extra bling. The sugar
   will dissolve well in the bath
   and leave your skin soft and
   refreshed!

Note:
For extra scent, I like to use rose
petal—scented witch hazel.

Vaya con Dios, my darlings!

Bonnie Parker Poetry Journal

A femme fatale with a penchant for fine fashion, on the FBI's Most Wanted list, a smoking hottie, *and* a poet? Heck, who wouldn't want to be Bonnie Parker? Well, most of us, actually. She and Clyde lived pretty rough, on the lam, sleeping in ditches, eating food straight from the can, getting shot up . . . Yet, between trips to the manicurist and weekend crime sprees, Parker found time to wax poetic. Even if you won't live the life of a moll, you can still write like one, with a handy handmade notebook complete with faux bullet holes.

SUPPLIES

Ruler or tape measure

Scissors or paper cutter

Brown paper bag or decorative scrapbook paper for cover

5 sheets of 8½ x 11-inch typing paper

Bone paper folder (optional)

Stapler

Glue stick

Small paintbrush

Red watercolor or tempera paint

Single-hole punch

The Trail's End

by Bonnie Parker

You've read the story of Jesse James
of how he lived and died.
If you're still in need;
of something to read,
here's the story of Bonnie and Clyde.

Now Bonnie and Clyde are the
    Barrow gang
I'm sure you all have read.
how they rob and steal;
and those who squeal,
are usually found dying or dead.

There's lots of untruths to these
    write-ups;
they're not as ruthless as that.
their nature is raw;
they hate all the law,
the stool pidgeons, spotters
    and rats.

They call them cold-blooded killers
they say they are heartless and mean.
But I say this with pride
that I once knew Clyde,
when he was honest and upright
    and clean.

But the law fooled around;
kept taking him down,
and locking him up in a cell.
Till he said to me;
"I'll never be free,
so I'll meet a few of them in hell"

The road was so dimly lighted
there were no highway signs to guide.
But they made up their minds;
if all roads were blind,
they wouldn't give up till they died.

The road gets dimmer and dimmer
sometimes you can hardly see.
But it's fight man to man
and do all you can,
for they know they can never
    be free.

From heart-break some people
    have suffered
from weariness some people
    have died.
But take it all in all;
our troubles are small,
till we get like Bonnie and Clyde.

If a policeman is killed in Dallas
and they have no clue or guide.
If they can't find a fiend,
they just wipe their slate clean
and hang it on Bonnie and Clyde.

There's two crimes committed
    in America
not accredited to the Barrow mob.
They had no hand;
in the kidnap demand,
nor the Kansas City Depot job.

A newsboy once said to his buddy;
"I wish old Clyde would get jumped.
In these awfull hard times;
we'd make a few dimes,
if five or six cops would get bumped"

The police haven't got the report yet
but Clyde called me up today.
He said, "Don't start any fights;
we aren't working nights,
we're joining the NRA."

From Irving to West Dallas viaduct
is known as the Great Divide.
Where the women are kin;
and the men are men,
and they won't "stool" on Bonnie
    and Clyde.

If they try to act like citizens
and rent them a nice little flat.
About the third night;
they're invited to fight,
by a sub-gun's rat-tat-tat.

They don't think they're too smart or
    desperate
they know that the law always wins.
They've been shot at before;
but they do not ignore,
that death is the wages of sin.

Some day they'll go down together
They'll bury them side by side.
To few it'll be grief,
To the law a relief
But it's death for Bonnie and Clyde

HOW TO

1. Measure and cut a $4\frac{1}{4}$ x 11-inch cover for your book from the brown paper bag or decorative paper.

2. Cut all five sheets of typing paper in half horizontally so they also measure $4\frac{1}{4}$ x 11 inches.

3. Fold each page in half to become $4\frac{1}{4}$ x $5\frac{1}{2}$ inches. Bone folders are a great tool for this step, as they make a sharp crease in your work.

4. Unfold the pages and stack them on top of the cover sheet.

5. Fold the packet in half; you should have a booklet measuring $4\frac{1}{4}$ x $5\frac{1}{2}$ inches.

6. Staple the booklet together as close as possible to the spine at the top, middle, and bottom of the journal.

7. Make a fancy label for your journal (by hand, or on the computer) and cut it out. Use a glue stick to attach it to the cover.

8. Dip a paintbrush in red paint and flick paint across the cover for a chilling blood-splatter effect.

9. With a pencil, lightly mark on the cover where you would like bullet holes to appear. Hole-punch the pencil markings.

10. Using the cover holes as a guide, pencil in holes on the first page of the book and punch again. Repeat this process through all the pages of your journal.

11. Compose a sonnet to yourself of love gone bad, life on the road, and hiding from Johnny Law.

iNViSiBLe INK

Of course, the poison pen is mightier than the dull-edged sword, and I've got a micro weapon of mass destruction. I write my manifestos in blood, plot bank jobs in ink black as midnight, but for secrets . . . well, those deserve a lighter touch. Like any clever spy, I like to hide things in plain sight, and invisible ink is just the trick. It is a cinch to whip up, and there are few things more delightful than a scorching-hot love note revealed over the bright flame of a candle.

As kids we made invisible ink using the juice of fresh-squeezed lemons. While practical, the mix doesn't store well and the ink can be a bit cloudy. This covert concoction is a clear upgrade.

SUPPLIES

Wide bowl

1 tablespoon citric acid powder (see Notes)

$\frac{1}{3}$ cup water

Metal-nib caligraphy pen

Light- or normal-weight typing or copy paper (heavy paper is harder to work with)

Small jar with a sealable lid

Candle and matches

HOW TO

1. In a wide bowl, combine the citric acid powder with the water. Stir until the mixture is no longer cloudy.

2. Dip the pen into the ink, pressing the nib down slightly. Write as usual, dipping the pen frequently--every three or four letters.

3. Transfer the ink to a small, lidded jar for storage and later use.

4. To decrypt: Hold the note over a candle flame close enough for the paper to brown but not catch fire--this will take some practice but is lots of fun in itself. It helps to know where the writing is on the paper before decrypting (see Notes).

5. Burn after reading.

Notes:

Citric acid is found in the canning section at grocery stores, or at health food stores, or online.

Consider making more than one copy of your final draft, in case the original note combusts during decryption (this can happen faster than you might think). Also, keep a glass of water nearby or decrypt next to a sink, just in case your writing becomes especially volatile.

"It's Your Funeral" Stamp Set

Graceful exits demand strategizing. The included templates are all the props needed to construct one last blowout, from flowers to headstones. The individual pieces make a lovely tabletop diorama or lightly veiled threat, should you decide to mail your ill will to "friends."

And since this is your funeral, why not go out in style? Could there be any cooler ride than the '61 Jaguar E-type that Bud Cort modifies into a hearse in the movie *Harold and Maude*? Go ahead, put on some Cat Stevens mood music, and while you're carving away, let your mind drift to the finer points of the afternoon, such as whom to leave out of the will and whether you'll have the punch spiked.

SUPPLIES

Heavyweight tracing paper

Soft linoleum for stamp carving

Linoleum-carving set

Black ink stamp pad

Scrap paper

Card stock

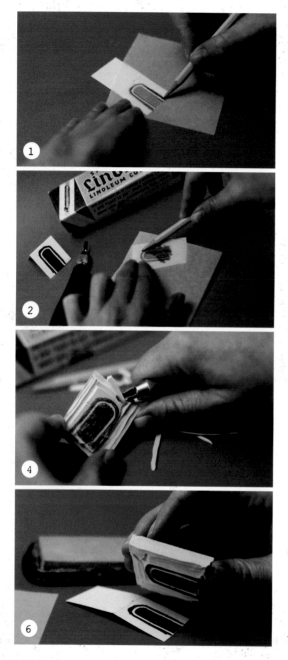

1. Use a pencil to trace the image from the template onto heavyweight tracing paper. If your pencil lines are light, darken them a few times with the pencil for a legible transfer.

2. Place the tracing paper, image side down, onto the linoleum. Rub the edge of a pencil horizontally across the back of the paper until the back of the drawing is covered completely with pencil and the image is transferred onto the linoleum.

3. Using the blade edge of the carving set, cut the outline of the drawing through about half the depth of the linoleum.

4. With the gouge edge of the carving set, remove the excess stamp material from outside the outline first, then carve out the white highlights of the stamp's interior spaces.

5. Apply ink to the stamp and test-drive the design on scrap paper. Add more highlights, if desired, and check one final time.

6. Stamp the images onto the front image area of the card stock (which is twice as high as the stamped design so you can fold it over).

7. Fold the card in half and plot out your plot.

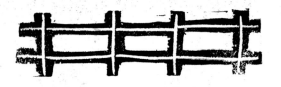

Finding Commonality

The following is a lexicon of words and phrases found in both the crafting and crime worlds. If you find yourself playing for both teams, as I often do, keep in mind context, as a word may have an entirely different meaning, depending on who is saying it.

-- Fleece
-- Frame
-- Whip stitch
-- Icing
-- Nailing
-- Laundering
-- Testing for doneness

-- Coming clean
-- Wax
-- Embellish
-- Stitch in the ditch
-- Plot
-- Plant
-- Carve

Grace Kelly's See-Behind Rear Window Shades

he kids accuse me of having eyes in the back of my head, and you know what? They're right. I've crafted up some stylish glasses with custom-fit wing mirrors, so I can look ahead of me and see who's checking out my ample assets in the rear.

These are super quick and easy to make. The most important part of this project is finding the right glasses to modify. First, you want something hip and fun—no sense leaving the house looking like a meff. Look for glasses with dark lenses and frames that are as flat as possible. If you place your mirror against a curved lens, you're going to get distorted circus-mirror images. Keep in mind that the bigger the frame, the more space you'll have for a mirror and a large field of vision behind you. Also, with big glasses you look like Edith Head—style points all around!

HOW TO

1. Gently lay the glasses face down onto some scrap paper and use a pencil to trace around the front of the frame.

2. On the scrap paper, measure your right frame area into thirds. Mark a vertical line one-third of the way from the outer edge of the frame. Repeat for the left side.

3. Cut out the template silhouette; discard the center piece.

4. Set the template on the back of the glasses and adjust it to fit on the frame. Depending on the frame style and fit, you may need to trim around the hinge area.

5. Trace the template onto the back of the mirror sheet and cut out.

6. Set the mirror pieces on the inside of the frame and tape temporarily in place.

7. Try on the glasses. You should be able to see in front clearly, and behind yourself as well; adjust the mirrors as needed. Use a grease pencil (or some tape) to mark the placement of the mirrors on the frame, then remove the mirrors from the glasses.

8. Layer hot glue onto the glasses frames where the mirrors will go and let it cool. *Don't put the mirrors on yet.* When the glue is cool, set the mirrors in place and check for fit. Can you see behind yourself? If yes, add another small layer of hot glue and immediately set the mirrors into place. If no, either break off the glue and try again, or build up more glue until the mirrors can be adjusted for rear viewing. Excess glue can be removed with an X-Acto knife once it has cooled.

Note:

The dark lenses hide the mirrors, so make sure you get lenses as black as possible. Avoid the mirrored ones, too. They make you look like a cop, and the idea here is to be in disguise, not give away the gag.

Case-the-Joint Craft Caddy

I'm in favor of organized crime. Like a good scout, I'm prepared for any crafting or drinking opportunity, with tools, mixers, and chasers neatly stored and at the ready. Suitcases are the obvious modus operandi, but the criminal crafter deserves a carryall worthy of malcontent.

Did the mob really pack tommy guns in violin cases? Heck, no! The cases are way too small, but it sure looks great in the movies. Here's how to customize your discarded suitcase or thrift store treasure into a multipurpose vehicle for holding martini glasses, a shaker, bottles of booze, a glue gun, glue sticks, paintbrushes, a craft knife, and anything else Eliot Ness might throw at you.

HOW TO

1. Rip the old liner out of the case. You may find some strange things under the original fabric, like wooden supports or foam lining. I pulled all this out, using a screwdriver to pry up stubborn pieces.

2. Lay a sheet of newspaper over the inside of the case. (Tape several pieces of newspaper together if you need enough to

SUPPLIES

Vintage luggage or violin case (see Notes)

Flat-head screwdriver--the kind without removable bits

Newspaper

Felt-tip marker

Scissors

Cardboard

Fabric for lining and pocket (see Notes)

Straight pins

Fabric chalk or washable fabric pen

Hot glue gun

1-inch-wide braided elastic and assorted elastic cords (see Notes)

Upholstery needle and thread (optional)

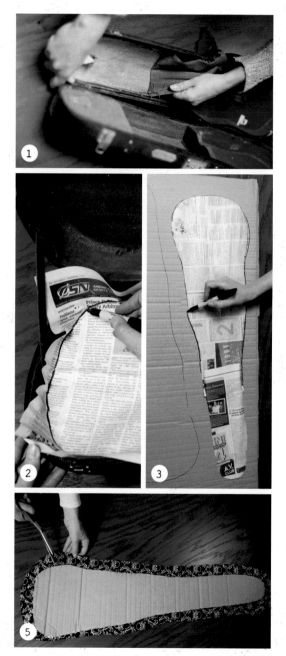

fit the entire length.) Press
the paper down and use a marker
to trace a line where the base
of the case meets the sides.
Take out the paper template and
cut along the traced line. Place
the template back in the case
and check the fit, adjusting as
necessary.

3. Lay the template on the
    cardboard and trace the shape.
    Cut out the cardboard insert.

4. Pin the paper template onto the
    fabric liner and, with fabric
    chalk or a washable fabric pen,
    trace a line around the entire
    shape 1 inch away from the
    original tracing line. This will
    give you extra material (a.k.a.
    selvage) around the edges to
    attach to the underside of the
    cardboard insert. Don't remove
    the template yet.

5. Cut 1-inch-long slits in
    the selvage area at 1-inch
    intervals. You may want to make
    additional slits where the
    pattern curves. This will keep
    the fabric from puckering and
    having strange folds when you
    glue it down.

6. Remove the pins and the paper
    template and lay the fabric
    right side (template side) down
    on your worktable. Then place
    the cardboard on top (on the
    wrong side of the fabric) and

glue down the fabric flaps around the edges, to fit the fabric to the cardboard snugly but without warping it.

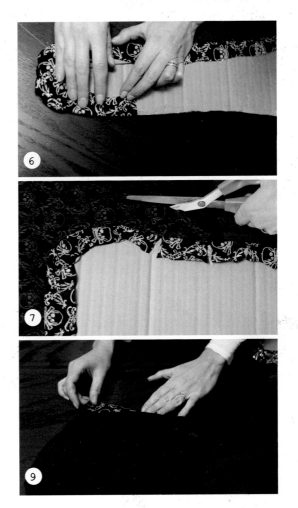

7. If you'd like to add a pocket to the bottom end of the case, place the pocket fabric wrong side up on your work surface, then lay the paper template or cardboard insert on the fabric right side down and trace around just the bottom, leaving a 1-inch allowance around the edges as you did in Step 4. Leave a ½-inch allowance at the top of the pocket so you can fold it over.

8. Cut the pocket piece from the fabric and cut 1-inch slits as you did in Step 5.

9. Fold the top ½ inch of the pocket over, wrong sides together, and glue it down. This will prevent fraying and leave a clean edge on the pocket.

10. Place the pocket right side down on your work surface and lay the cardboard on top with the fabric side down.

11. Glue the pocket selvage seams down onto the back of the cardboard (over where the main fabric selvages have been glued).

12. I use elastic cords and straps to hold down plastic martini glasses and small flasks. Determine where you'd like to place them. I've found it helpful to put all my crafting and drinking supplies into the case first and draw a map on my paper template.

13. Glue the elastic straps into place, folding over an inch of the excess at each edge and gluing it to the back side of the cardboard.

14. Secure the cords with firm knots on the back side of the cardboard and use an upholstery needle to stitch through the cardboard and fabric. An extra daub of hot glue will reinforce the knot and will keep it from pulling through to the other side.

15. Once the new liner is completely assembled it can be hot glued into the base of your case.

Notes:

I found my violin case for next to nothing at a shop that sells used instruments, and there are always great deals online.

Pretty much anything goes for the fabric lining, from cotton to fake fur. Since I'm a messy crafter and a sloppy drinker, I looked for a pattern where stains wouldn't be too noticeable. You might want to treat the fabric with Scotchgard or another protectant before mounting it into the case, if you'd like to minimize wear. I also like to buy enough fabric to make a pocket.

The elastic cords hold my bottles, glasses, and brushes in place. I used less than a yard of each in my project, but I always buy extra when I'm at the craft store, as I never know when I'll have to bind something quickly (or gag it, for that matter!).

What to pack

Outfitting your kit is a
super treat--I like to have
a sewing kit with scissors,
the indispensable glue gun,
an extension cord, markers,
paints, brushes, maps, train
schedules, fake passport,
margarita salt, absinthe,
lock pick . . . you know,
the usual . . .

Pulp Fiction Pendant

Like a true romantic, I've been accused of wearing my heart on my sleeve and my smut dangling tantalizingly on a silver chain twined around my milky throat, delicious spare inches from my plunging neckline and trembling, buxom . . . oh, you get the picture.

My passions run deep, from noir jewelry accessories to trashy detective novels. And while I'm deeply enamored of the titillating verbiage and sleazy plot devices of '50s and '60s pulp fiction, it's really the salacious cover art that makes my blood boil. The scantily clad, pop art femme fatales look stunning on this DIY choker; the supplies are super inexpensive; and best of all, you'll have a great excuse to add a few more bombshells to your collection of racy reads.

SUPPLIES

Titillating pulp fiction novel with a great cover

1¼-inch-high by ¾-inch-wide recessed pendant base (see Sources)

Clear packing tape

Scissors

Glue stick

Resin epoxy sealer (see Note)

Straight pin

Necklace chain and clasp (see Sources)

HOW TO

1. Take your favorite smarmy pulp novel to the copy shop (or use a home computer and scanner) and reduce the image size to fit inside the pendant frame.

2. Lay a strip of clear tape over the top of the printed image, pressing down firmly to get out any air bubbles. Many printer inks will bleed when the clear sealer is added, and the tape on top will protect your image from running.

3. Cut out your design and use a glue stick to tack it down into the pendant. This step is very important. Your paper art might float to the top of the sealer or have an uneven surface if it isn't glued down and allowed to dry first.

4. Follow the manufacturer's directions for applying the resin sealer on top of the pulp art. Use a small pin to poke out any air holes in the sealant.

5. Wait 24 hours for the pendant to dry, and don it on your favorite chain, you saucy minx, you!

Note:

I like to use Glossy Accents, a "clear dimensional embellishment sealer" (see Sources) because there is no mixing involved and it magnifies my images once the sealer dries.

Shiv Cozy

H ey, Lola—is that a knife in your skirt, or are you
happy to see me?

Here's how to craft up a stylish hands-free
carryall for your concealed weapon of choice. The
polar fleece sheath holds a blade five inches in
length and can be sewn or constructed with a glue
gun. A rhinestone strand and skull embellishments
give the cozy a detailed, feminine touch. Made from
sequined elastic, the garter stretches around your
devilishly sexy upper thigh, keeping your little secret
safely tucked away.

SUPPLIES

Heavyweight tracing paper

Straight pins

1/4 yard polar fleece

Scissors

X-Acto knife

Hot glue gun

14-inch-long plastic
   rhinestone strand or other
   beading

7-inch-long piece decorative
   ribbon trim

2-inch-wide piece stretch
   sequined elastic
   approximately 22 inches in
   length, or enough to fit
   snugly around your thigh
   with a 1-inch overlap for
   seams

HOW TO

1. Copy the shiv cozy pattern onto
    heavyweight tracing paper and pin it to
    the polar fleece.

2. Using the template as a guide, cut out
    the front and back of the cozy.

3. Using an X-Acto knife, cut vertical slits
    where indicated on the back of the cozy.

4. Hot glue the rhinestone string or other
    decorative beading to the front panel of
    the cozy.

5. Using a ⅛-inch seam allowance, glue or sew the front and back pieces of the cozy together with the wrong sides of the fleece facing, leaving the top open.

6. Glue the decorative ribbon around the top of the cozy, overlapping in the back.

7. Pass the sequined garter through the back slits of the cozy as if through a belt loop.

8. Check the garter for snug fit before sewing the overlapping ends together. Open up the seam allowance and sew down the sides for a tailored look and extra durability.

9. Because it is made from polar fleece, the cozy isn't recommended for everyday use; but it makes a stunning costume accessory, or it can carry less dangerous objects, such as lipstick, a cell phone, bail money, or pinking shears.

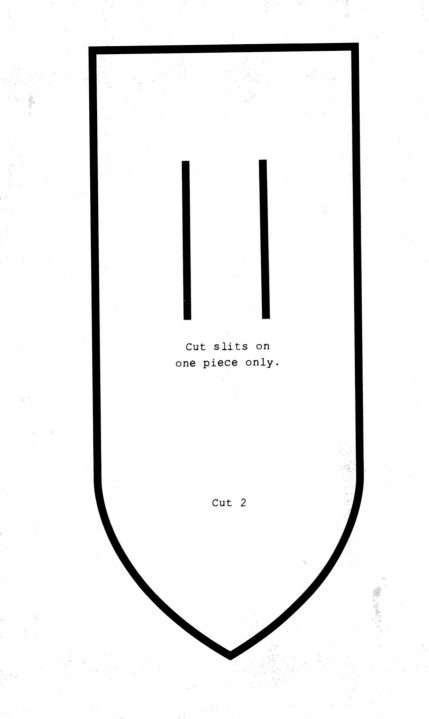

Cut slits on
one piece only.

Cut 2

HELL iN A HANDBAG

I hate being frisked, preferring to be on the business end of shakedowns instead. I do like to keep my little secrets, though, and a large purse with a false bottom is certainly convenient when you've got to tote "personal items" around town. It won't fool a fancy security machine, but if you want to sneak a flask into the movies, this is the handbag for you.

You'll need to do a little sewing for this project, though a resourceful crafter could also make the seams using a glue gun or an iron and fusible bonding tape.

The first time I made this bag I used industrial-weight Velcro to attach the false liner to the inside of my purse. Conceptually, it was a brilliant idea—I was able to easily access a trove of goodies from the hidden depths of the bag, just like a magic clown car. Unfortunately, the highly audible tearing sound of Velcro being plied apart totally gave me away! Boy, was my probation officer displeased. My newly modified false liner is constructed from sturdy cotton fabric, glue, and blessedly silent magnetic tape for attaching fabric to the inside of the purse.

SUPPLIES

Handbag

Hot glue gun

Magnetic tape (see Sources)

Fabric measuring tape

Fabric for liner (see Note)

Scissors

Sewing machine, or needle and thread

Fabric marker

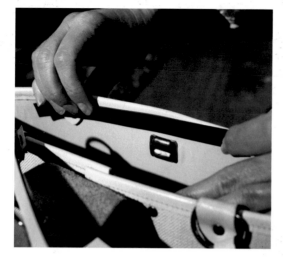
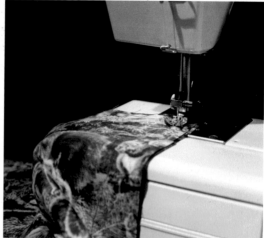

HOW TO

1. Rip or cut out the original purse liner.

2. Hot glue a strip of magnetic tape around the top edge of the interior of the purse opening.

3. Use the fabric measuring tape to take the interior dimensions of the bag--height and width. To calculate your new liner size, use your original width dimension but add 1 inch for the seam allowances. Because you'll want the new liner to be shorter than the original, measure the new length one-third shorter than the original dimension, plus $\frac{1}{2}$ inch for the seam allowance at the bottom. For example, my purse measures 18 inches tall on the inside, so my new liner is $12\frac{1}{2}$ inches tall. Cut out the fabric liner.

4. Place the right sides of the fabric together and stitch the side and bottom seams, leaving a $\frac{1}{2}$-inch seam allowance all around, sewing twice to reinforce the seam.

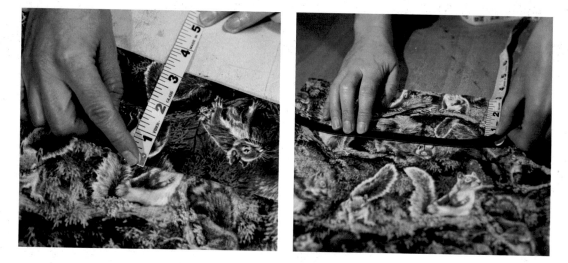

5. Mark a hemline on the wrong sides of the top of the liner. I went for an extra-long 3-inch hem, which in retrospect was ridiculous. A 1-inch hem will work just fine as long as there is enough fabric to fold over the magnetic tape.

6. Hot glue the magnetic tape around the inside of the hemline.

7. When the glue is cool, fold the upper part of the liner over the tape.

8. Put the liner inside the purse, letting the magnetic tape of the liner and bag meet through the fabric. The tape will be strong enough to allow you to stow all your gear in the main compartment, while still sliding apart easily and quietly when you want to access the secret area underneath.

Note:

Look for a fabric that is durable and that will complement your handbag. I chose a busy squirrel motif, which made my empty bag seem fuller, and is fairly distracting by its own merits. Plus, I like squirrels. Next to raccoons, they are the biggest thieves in the forest.

Pimp-My-Bank-Job Mexican Wrestler Ski Mask

is your balaclava looking a little tattered around the edges? Maybe your crew isn't throwing down the proper respect you're due. Bring on the bling, baby—a little satin and sequins on that winter mask and they'll be calling you "El Bandito," the perp of mystery, a hood to be reckoned with.

You can use the template provided or let your imagination run wild, creating luchador personas for all the gang—El Guapo, Tía Diabla, Carta Blanca—the possibilities are endless. At the next big heist, they won't be looking at your face, but admiring your crazy loco style.

SUPPLIES

Scissors

Straight pins

Craft felt (see Notes)

Sequins, beads, feathers, glitter, glitter glue—bust it *all* out! This project screams for overembellishing.

Hot glue gun (see Notes)

Full-face "robber-style" ski mask (see Notes)

HOW TO

1. Enlarge the template from the book 120 percent or to fit your mask.

2. Cut out the template and pin it to the felt.

3. Cut out the felt and embellish it with sequins, glitter, and other craft accessories.

4. Glue the decorated felt and other ornaments to the mask. Do *not* try on the mask until the glue is completely dry and cool. The last thing you want to do is blister your pretty mug!

Notes:

This is a great project for using up colorful remnants from your scrap felt bin. You'll need a full $8\frac{1}{2}$ x 11-inch sheet of felt for the included template.

A patient crafter *could* choose to sew the decorative bits to the wrestling mask, but if you're in a hurry, like me, with Interpol hot on your tail, well then, the instant gratification of the glue gun makes it the weapon of choice.

These wool balaclavas are very inexpensive--under $10 at most army surplus stores. While my taste runs to classic black, camouflage hats would make excellent wrestling masks, as well.

Luchador Name Generator

I've so many pseudonyms going, you'd think I had a personality disorder. While coming up with the perfect alias is a treat for me, other punks in my crew find it a real brain buster. To keep my posse fresh for bigger things and to ensure everyone gets a fair deal in the a.k.a. business, I came up with a wrestling-themed name generator. We may be crooks, but this is a democracy, with me as the evil El Jefe . . .

First, your friends will need to choose a prefix from the following: El, La, The, Tía, Tío, Dr., Judge, General, Don, Captain, Master, Commander, Mr., Mrs., Royal, Professor, Professora, Maestro, His Holiness . . .

Write down the following monikers on slips of paper. Names from column #1 should go in a jar or hat marked #1; names from column #2, in jar #2. If your crew is anything like mine, you'll want to fold the slips in half so there is no peeking. Draw your fate.

Column #1

Delicioso/a	Penitent	Unlucky
Lucky	Pequeño/a	Puerco
Loco/a	Erupting	Metallico/a
Grumpy	Nuclear	Luchador
Giganto/a	Caliente	Nacho
Bodacious	Tijuana	Rapido/a
Sangre	Raging	Bonita
Diabolical	Mejor	Fiery
Silente	Gordo	Atomic
Rey	Brujo/a	Bambino/a
Bashful	Burping	Stupido/a
Complacent	Spicy	Stinky
Dulce	Bandito/a	Destructo/a
Angelica	Guapo/a	Magnifico/a
Ultimo/a	Lazy	Superior
Bizarro/a	Tamale	Liquado/a
Flatulent	Audacious	

Column #2

Mostacho	Butcher	Sausage
Cobra	Dragon	Taco
Hombre	Wasp	Bacon
Stinky Pants	Quesadilla	Hurricane
Interrupter	Cannibal	Mezzo Forte
Underpants	Ambassador	Santo/a
Tigre	Pistole	Hooligan
Jaguar	Prince/	Defibulator
Perro	Princess	Mariachi
Luchador	Interloper	Vampiro/a
Pontifica	Federale	Chinchilla
Bug	Padre/Madre	Brute
Ventriloquist	Squirrel	Neglecter
Capitalist	Diablo/a	Zapata
Monstruo	Tortilla	Roboto
Fajita	Chihuahua	Scorpion
Skeleton	Legend	Mysterioso/a
Spinster	Tormentor	Administrator
Volcano	Chimichanga	Cerveza
Cupid	Guerrilla	Steamroller
Amigo/a	Margarita	Chupacabra
Bride/Groom	Destructor	

Enlarge 120 percent

Hangman's Noose Finger-Knit Belt

Sometimes your access to supplies and equipment is severely hindered, such as when you're traveling, or in solitary. Don't let the man hold you down! Whipping together this mortal coil is a cinch! I used fancy yarn, but you could always deconstruct some thick socks or a woolly sweater for this swinging accessory. No needles are required, just a few nimble fingers and yarn.

The versatile belt can double as a scarf or perhaps you can find other uses for it. With a little practice, a long belt can be thrown together in less than an hour.

SUPPLIES

1 skein chunky yarn
Five fingers
Yarn needle

HOW TO

1. Lay the yarn across your fingers as shown in the photo: over your pinkie, under your ring finger, over your middle finger, under your index finger. The tail end of your yarn should extend a few inches past your pinkie.

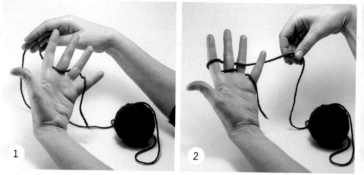

1. 2.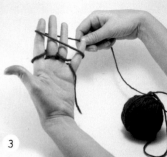

2. To make the second row of knitting, wrap the yarn forward around the front of your index finger, under the middle finger, in front of your ring finger, and under your pinkie.

3. Wrap the yarn around to the front of your pinkie and lay it across all four fingers, above the weaving (this is your *working* thread).

4. Starting with your index finger, lift the bottom loop up over your working thread and push your index finger up into the loop.

4a

5. Repeat this step with your middle, ring, and pinkie fingers--lifting the loop up over the working thread, and inserting each finger into the hole.

6. Lift the tail end of your pinkie thread up over the pinkie loop and place it at the back of your hand.

7. Your working thread should be at the back of your hand, behind your index finger. Bring the thread behind all your fingers toward your pinkie and wrap it to the front, toward your index finger, above the loops, as you did in Step 3.

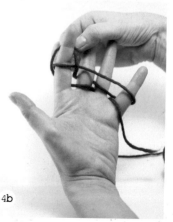

4b

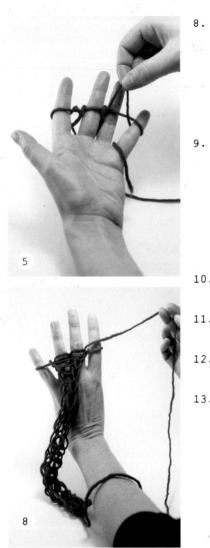

8. Repeat Steps 3 through 7 until the work has reached your desired length. During the knitting process, you'll occasionally need to tighten your work. Pull gently at the finished loops at the back of your working hand and the stitches will come neatly together.

9. When you are ready to get the loops off your fingers, pull the yarn about 22 inches from your hand and cut it. Thread the end of this yarn through the four loops on your fingers. Remove the loops from your fingers and pull tight on the tail. Leave the tail in place-- you'll use this piece to make the hangman's knot.

10. Lay the belt on a flat surface and make a fold in the belt 8 inches from the end.

11. Wrap the tail piece around both sections of the belt ten times.

12. Thread the tail onto a yarn needle and sew the yarn under the wrapped sections.

13. While this also makes a fetching scarf or trendy necklace, I would strongly encourage you *not* to wear it too tight.

Glue Gun Bandolier

Want to shout out to the world that you are a badass crafter? This super fashionable belt can be worn around your chest in true Zapata revolutionary style, or wrapped around your waist, putting glue sticks within easy reach for rapid-fire craft action. As you'll be using a lot of hot glue to craft up this li'l gem, it's a pay-to-play project, highlighting your skills as a true craftista.

SUPPLIES

Seat belt strapping or other webbing (see Sources)

Scissors

Measuring tape

Chalk

Hot glue gun

Glue sticks

Military belt buckle or strap fasteners, also known as metal slides (see Sources)

HOW TO

1. Measure the length of the webbing, prom queen—sash style, starting with the top of your shoulder, then going down diagonally across your chest, under your arm to the back side, and up diagonally across your back, the ends meeting again at the top of your shoulder with some additional room left to adjust the belt. My belt measures 55 inches.

2. Cut a second, 30-inch strip of webbing, which will be used to secure the glue sticks to the belt. Set it aside.

3. Lay the longer piece of webbing diagonally across your chest in bandito fashion. With chalk, mark the point where the belt meets the top of your collarbone.

4. Spread out the belt on a flat surface. Hot glue 1 inch of the shorter webbing to the belt piece at the chalk line. Fold the shorter webbing away from the bottom piece and place the glue stick on the belt where the two pieces meet. It should fit snugly between the belt pieces.

5. Make a line of hot glue directly next to the glue stick, making sure the glue is as close to the stick as possible so the pieces don't fall out of your holster during vigorous craft/revolution settings.

6. Fold the top webbing down to the glue, securing the stick between the belt pieces.

7. Repeat Steps 4 through 6 for each stick until all pieces have been attached.

8. Fit the buckle pieces onto the belt and don it with pride.

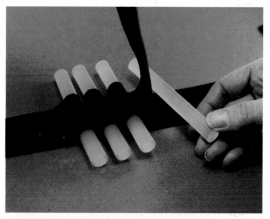

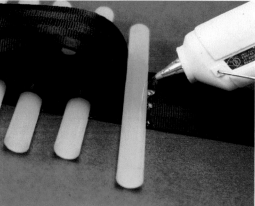

CRIME SCENE TAPE MESSENGER BAG

SUPPLIES

3 to 4 paper bags

Measuring tape

Scissors

2 rolls yellow duct tape

Bubble Wrap

Crime scene tape (see
  Sources, also available
  online at law enforcement
  supply stores--seriously!)

Clear packing tape

Black construction paper

Glue stick

You can tell a lot about people by what they wear, and my accessories are usually "after the fact." Creeping around in all kinds of weather, I demand a carryall that can take a beating, is water-resistant, and is roomy enough for surveillance equipment, a couple of cheap novels, a disguise kit, lipsticks, and a sandwich. Of course, it's got to be stainproof, and if I can wipe my prints down with a quick spritz of window cleaner, all the better. Finding a dream bag that fit the bill was more of a chore than ditching my last husband. Like so many other things in life, if I wanted the job done right, I had to do it myself.

Fortunately, creating a custom bag is lots of fun, and duct tape has become my medium of choice. It's super strong and has that rugged "don't mess with me" vibe, "This *is* duct tape, and, clearly, I know how to use it." Just to make my intentions clear, I've fashioned my shoulder strap from standard-issue CSI tape. They call it a "messenger bag" for a reason! From crime spree to shopping spree, this is the perfect tote for a standard-size laptop, getaway accessories, and all your other damaged goods.

HOW TO

1. Open up a paper bag and cut it in half at the vertical seams. Remove and recycle the bottom panel of the bag.

2. Cut a 12 x 16½-inch piece of the brown paper for the front panel of the bag. Lay horizontal strips of duct tape across one side of the paper, slightly overlapping each row, to create a base layer of tape for the messenger bag.

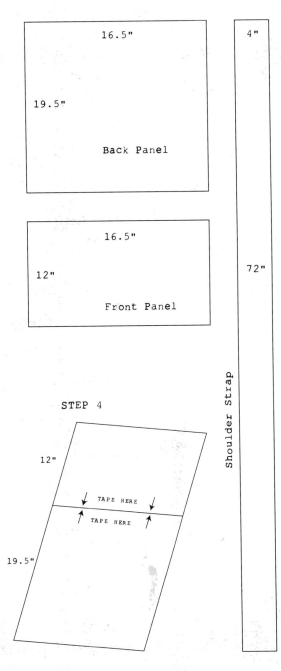

16.5"

19.5"

Back Panel

16.5"

12"

Front Panel

STEP 4

12"

↓ TAPE HERE ↓
↑ TAPE HERE ↑

19.5"

4"

72"

Shoulder Strap

3. Deconstruct a second paper bag for the back panel of the bag. This time you'll need to use paper patched together from both the front and back sections of the paper bag, to create a panel piece that measures $19\frac{1}{2}$ x $16\frac{1}{2}$ inches. Slightly overlap the bag sections and tape them in place. Again, lay horizontal tape stripes to finish covering one side of the bag panel piece.

4. Tape the front and back panels together, creating one long piece of material that measures $31\frac{1}{2}$ x $16\frac{1}{2}$ inches.

5. Tape Bubble Wrap to the side of the bag that isn't covered with duct tape. Cover the Bubble Wrap layer with the yellow duct tape.

6. Tape together scrap pieces from the two deconstructed paper bags to create a strip 72 inches long and 4 inches wide. Cover the underside of the paper arm strap with yellow duct tape.

7. Center the 3-inch-wide crime scene tape on top of the arm strap. Use yellow duct tape to hold the crime scene tape in place, slightly overlapping the top and bottom $1/4$ inch of the crime scene tape and folding the duct tape over onto the back side of the strap. Cover the crime scene tape entirely with clear packing tape to keep it from tearing.

8. Tape the arm strap to the vertical edges of the front panel.

9. Tape the bottom of the arm strap edges to the bottom of the back panel.

10. Tape the arm strap to the back panel. Starting at the bottom edges of the arm strap, tape 12 inches up toward the top. The remainder of this panel is your overlapping front flap.

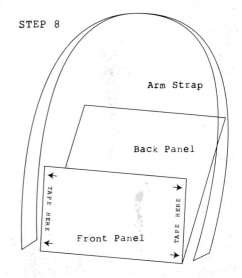

STEP 8

Arm Strap

Back Panel

TAPE HERE

TAPE HERE

Front Panel

11. To reinforce your bag, tape the inside of the arm strap seams as well.

12. Enlarge the body outline design template to your desired size and cut it out. Trace it onto black construction paper and cut it out.

13. Lay the design on the bag. If it overlaps onto the front flap, cut it in half and glue half to the flap and half to the bag, as shown in the photo.

14. Cover the design with clear packing tape to protect it.

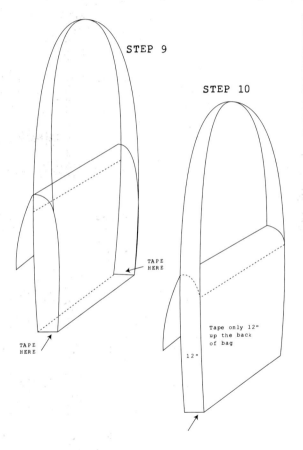

STEP 9

STEP 10

TAPE HERE

TAPE HERE

Tape only 12" up the back of bag

12"

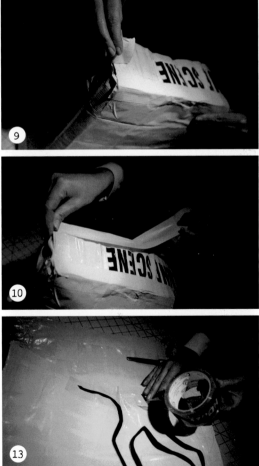

Martha's No-Knit Prison Poncho

In the wee hours of March 4, 2005, Martha Stewart walked out of Alderson Federal Prison Camp a free woman, her debt to society paid. Snapshots showed her boarding a private jet in a gorgeous gray-and-cream crocheted poncho made for her by fellow inmate Xiomara Hernandez (see Sources). The poncho became an overnight sensation. Web sites featuring interpretations of the pattern crashed from user overload, and collector replicas are still fetching high bids on online auctions.

My homage to the grand vizier of craft cuts a few corners; in fact, there is no knitting or crocheting involved, just two seams on the sewing machine. Warm enough for a Connecticut winter, the fleece poncho is constructed in a "work party orange" color with a black-and-white striped liner for that "bustin' out of the joint" look. Detailed embellishments include a hand-stamped ribbon with Martha's prison number and fierce metal grommet holes around the neckline. M. Diddy—this one's for you!

SUPPLIES

- 45-inch-square piece black-and-white striped cotton fabric
- Hot glue gun or fusible fabric tape
- 5½ yards (1-inch-wide) orange grosgrain ribbon
- Scissors
- Fabric chalk
- 48-inch-square piece orange polar fleece
- Straight pins
- Needle (or sewing machine) and orange sewing thread
- 10 (³⁄₈-inch) silver metal grommets
- 2¼ yards black elastic cording
- Numerical rubber stamps or small stencils
- Permanent stamp ink or fabric paint
- 6-inch-wide white cotton ribbon trim for prisoner ID number

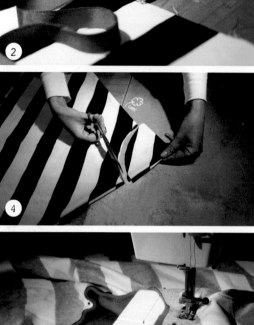

HOW TO

1. Lay the striped fabric liner on a flat surface, right side up.

2. Using a glue gun or fusible fabric tape, attach the grosgrain ribbon to all four sides of the poncho liner. The ribbon should extend horizontally $\frac{1}{2}$ inch beyond each edge of the fabric to create a decorative trim edge. Let the glue cool.

3. Fold the poncho liner in half, the top edge folding down to meet the bottom edge. Fold in half again with the left edge coming over to meet the right.

4. Pin the neck hole template to the upper left corner of the fabric square. Use fabric chalk to trace the template. Cut out the neck hole.

5. Repeat Steps 3 and 4 on the polar fleece layer.

6. Pin the fleece layer and the lining together at the neck opening. The lining should be print side down on top of the fleece.

7. Sew the neck seam with a $\frac{3}{4}$-inch seam allowance.

8. Cut triangular notches every inch around the neck seam to ease the fabric tension.

9. Flip the fabric right side out so the insides of the poncho meet. Adjust the liner at the neck so it can't be seen from the outside.

10. Stitch a ¼-inch topstitch around the neck of the poncho on the right sides of the fabric for a neatly finished edge.

11. Lay out the poncho on your worktable and mark the grommet holes. I eyeballed this step, but for a uniform look, space the grommets every 4½ inches. The grommets should measure 1½ inches from the top of the neck seam.

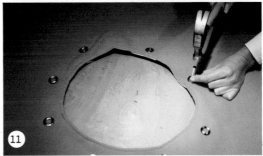

12. Follow the manufacturer's directions for attaching your particular brand of grommet to the poncho.

13. Lace the elastic cord through the grommet holes.

14. Use rubber stamps and a permanent fabric ink to write your prisoner ID insignia on the white ribbon trim. Stencils or embroidery would work well for this finishing step, too.

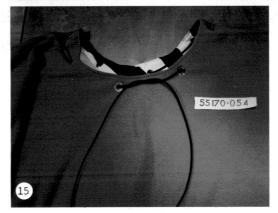

15. Glue your ID number to the front of the poncho. I, of course, picked out the perfect number for my poncho: 55170-054, Martha's number when she went away.

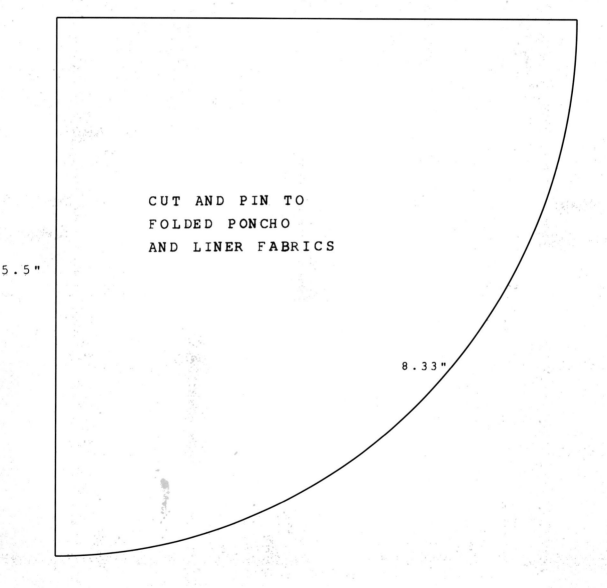

5.5"

5.5"

CUT AND PIN TO
FOLDED PONCHO
AND LINER FABRICS

8.33"

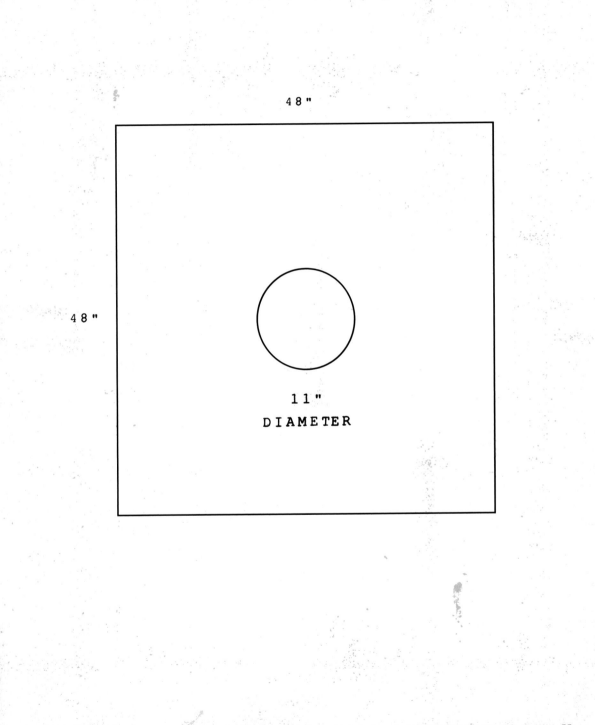

Mom's Cake with a File Inside

i come from a long line of mischievous women. My mom's criminal record is a magnum opus, taking up a full filing cabinet in the spare room. The last time she got herself thrown in the clink, I decided to put my foot down. No more kissing away good money on bail when she's going to skip town anyway. Better to let Mom cool her heels for a couple of days and find her own way home. I'm not a totally heartless child (don't want to be written out of the will completely), so I made her this fabulosa cake with the quintessential file hidden inside.

I've never actually tried to make a jailbreak with a file, but I've seen it done in movies, so I'm fairly certain it should work. A fault with this end of the product will not result in a refund for this book. My durable metal file is about six inches in length, wrapped in a tidy parchment paper seal, stealthily hidden in the upper cake layer after baking.

Due to their sweet nature and natural decoy of being a food product, cakes really are a great vehicle for hiding all sorts of things. My favorite thing to hide? Cell phones. Carefully wrapped in a plastic bag, a hidden phone is a deliciously devious way to sing "Happy Birthday," when, due to unforeseen circumstances or a restraining order, you can't be there in person.

SUPPLIES

Favorite box cake mix

Two 8- or 9-inch cake pans

Favorite premade frosting

Awesome object you'd like to hide--file, phone, keys to the vault, handcuffs, directions to the secret lair . . .

Parchment or waxed paper

HOW TO

1. Follow the directions on the box for mixing and baking a double-layer cake. Let the cakes cool completely on a cooling rack.

2. Put the bottom layer of the cake on a serving plate and cover it with a layer of frosting.

3. For hiding large objects, cut a wedge from the top layer of the cake. The wedge should be slightly larger in width than the object you wish to hide. (To hide small, flat objects like files, you don't need to make a hidden compartment. Just wrap the file in parchment or waxed paper, stealthily slide it horizontally into the middle of the top cake layer, place the top layer on the bottom, and finish frosting.)

4. Carve a hidden pocket in the wedge area by making a horizontal slit 1 inch from the top of the cake and another 1 inch from the bottom. Use a paring knife to make a small vertical cut 1 inch from the side to remove the piece.

5. Wrap your secret treasure in plastic and put it into the cake cavity.

6. Put the top layer of cake on top of the bottom (frosted) layer. Slide the wedge back into the cake.

7. Frost the sides and top of the cake with enough icing to make sure your deception is completely hidden.

In high school, Mom ditched all her home ec classes in favor of jacking cars in the faculty parking lot. While she can slip off cuffs faster than Houdini and never met a safe she couldn't crack, my mom can't bake to save her soul. Since we're using her recipe here, it's about as simple as possible while still getting away with the moniker of "homemade."

Absinthe Makes the Heart Grow Fonder

I know where the bodies are buried; at least I should, because I put them there. Lately, though, I've been a bit forgetful, and fear I've misplaced hairy Harry. I'll put it down to long nights of "historical research" intently studying the little green fairies at the bottom of an absinthe glass.

Revelers who've consumed too much claim hazy visions of phantasms and spritely spirits, shortly before passing out. This bad reputation caused absinthe to be banned in the United States from 1915 until 2007. Now that absinthe is legal again, the good stuff is pretty easy to find.

Harder to locate is the requisite absinthe spoon, a flat, slotted utensil that sits atop your glass, holding liquor-infused sugar cubes that are set alight. The proper drinking and presentation of absinthe is essential if you don't want to be mistaken for a neophyte. Converted dinner forks make an endearing hostess gift that should be remembered long after the recipients have drifted off to a fuzzy green stupor, and a little prodding with this device may help to jog their memories of the evening when they come to, days later.

SUPPLIES

(Serves 1)

Fork

Hammer

Thin-gauge wire (see Note; see Sources)

Wire cutters

Glass tumbler or martini glass

1 sugar cube

2 shots absinthe

Match

4 shots distilled water

Ice (optional)

HOW TO

1. Lay the fork on a hard surface, such as a concrete floor, and hammer it flat.

2. Starting at the bottom of the fork, weave the wire over and under each tine, wrapping around the outer ends until the work reaches the tips. Snip the wire, leaving a 1-inch tail, and weave the tail back into the fork.

3. For extra embellishment, I include a band of wire around the neck of my fork. Lay one end of wire along the narrowest part of the fork, then wrap the bands over the loose end. When your band is at the desired length, tuck the finished end under the bands at the underside of the fork.

4. To serve: Set the absinthe spoon--or, in your case, fork--across the top of the glass and put one sugar cube on top. Pour two shots of absinthe onto the sugar, letting the excess seep into the glass.

5. Set the cube on fire and let the sugar foam and caramelize slightly. Drop the sugar into the absinthe and stir.

6. Add 4 shots of water and stir again. Your drink will take on a lovely opalescence. Serve straight up or add ice.

Note:
Colored wire can be found in many hues at craft stores.

AtOMiC CHeRRY BOMb

SUPPLIES

(Serves 1)

Pop Rocks (red matches the
    drink, but other colors are
    fun, too)

Martini glass

Lemon or lime wedge

Cocktail shaker

Ice

2 shots Kirschwasser

Lemon-lime soda

Fireball jawbreaker

Some notable spies like their drinks a fussy way—"shaken, not stirred." You know how I like my drinks? Exploding! Show some chest hair, man! I want enough booze to knock my feet out from under me, and a little something special that will start a party in my mouth.

Secretly developed by the East Germans during the cold war, the Atomic Cherry Bomb is rimmed in rapid-fire Pop Rocks action. A splash of lemon-lime soda is added to ice-cold Kirschwasser (a cherry brandy), and the whole thing is garnished with a fiery-hot jawbreaker. The drink starts with a clear glassy hue, and as the fireball slowly dissolves in a mushroom-cloudy fizz, the Atomic Cherry Bomb takes on a shade of deep Communist red, and a sizzling cinnamon taste.

HOW TO

1. Pour the Pop Rocks onto a shallow dish
    slightly larger than the rim of your
    glass.

2. Rub the lemon or lime wedge around the
    rim of your glass, squeezing out a little
    juice as you go.

3. Dredge the martini glass in the Pop Rocks. You'll want to move quickly from here on, as your drink will become volatile at this point.

4. Fill a cocktail shaker with ice.

5. Pour 2 shots of Kirschwasser over the ice. Cover the shaker, and shake several times to a catchy rhythm ("Shave and a Haircut" is a personal favorite).

6. Strain into the martini glass and top off with soda.

7. Drop the bomb and wait for the magic. The mushroom-cloud effect usually sets off about 30 seconds after the candy has been deployed into the drink. The longer the fireball sits, the darker the drink gets, though the Pop Rocks tend to mellow after a few minutes. Ideally, you'll want to taste this treat in several stages, like a rocket booster.

MUG Shot

My buddy Pooch is a walking encyclopedia of criminal lore—knows his Miranda like the back of his hand, probably because he's heard it enough times. He can spot a grifter with dummy twenties before the guy's even opened his wallet. Pooch is a decent bartender, and a good pal to have in a knife fight. You'd think with all his time in the clink he'd be better at board games and dice, but maybe he lets me win to keep me coming around.

The other day he fixed me up the house drink, the Mug Shot—strong cardamom coffee slammed back with a shot of sambuca. He told me that back in the old days, in Sicily, you might see this flaming liqueur served with a couple of espresso beans floating on top, symbolic of health and happiness. If your waiter gave you a drink with three beans, it was the signal for a hit about to go down and you'd best settle the tab and clear out quick.

Pooch had this faraway look in his eye as he related this particular anecdote. *Plip, plip.* I watched the beans drop softly into my glass, and as he let the third one go . . . I dropped to the deck. Pooch was fast; they were faster.

Bullets ripped through the place, and when the smoke cleared, my friend wasn't looking so good.

SUPPLIES

(Serves 1)

Coffee grinder

Dark roast coffee or espresso beans (see Notes)

Whole cardamom seeds (see Notes)

Coffeemaker or French press

Tall, wide coffee mug

Shot glass

2 ounces sambuca

2 or 3 whole espresso beans

Match

With his dying breath he whispered, "Someday, someday . . ." A plea for vengeance . . . or was he calling out a last seven-letter Scrabble move . . . with nowhere to play it?

To honor Pooch's memory, I've included the recipe here, but with upgrades. These days, I light my shot on fire, drop it straight in the coffee, and chug them both together quick—because you never know. And I tip my waitress 20 percent, just to hedge my bets.

HOW TO

1. In a coffee grinder, combine the coffee beans and cardamom seeds.

2. Brew the coffee in an automatic maker or French press.

3. Fill the coffee mug about three-quarters full. You'll want to use a tall mug for this and one wide enough to drop the shot glass down into. You may want to practice this step over the sink a few times, first using only water in both your mug and shot glass, to make sure you don't cause an overflow or other collateral damage.

4. Fill a shot glass with sambuca and whole espresso beans--two beans for friends, three for "less than friends."

5. Light the shot on fire.

6. Grab your shot glass down low (the rim area is getting pretty hot), drop the shot glass straight down into the coffee, and drink up.

7. Look for the back door while you're finishing this round.

Notes:

I suggest brewing a 6-cup pot of coffee. It may be more than you need, but it should be enough to fill even the largest mug.

The general rule for measuring ground coffee is 2 tablespoons of ground coffee per 6 ounces (¾ cup) of water. When making my ground coffee blend, I estimate one whole cardamom seed for every two cups of brewed coffee. So for a 6-cup pot, you'd need 3 whole seeds.

Crime Scene Gingerbread Men

"*r*un, run as fast as you can . . . ." Ooh! Not fast enough! Each of these junior G-men has met a very cruel demise, served on an individual plate with a black body outline.

Time for you to play mad baker, beat the eggs, whip the cream, practice your half-hitch knot in the licorice ropes, and ice the wee men once and for all. The cookies taste as good as they look, and by evening's end, the only evidence left will be a pile of crumbs. My recipe deviates from the traditional standbys with a kick of liquor for a good old-fashioned rum punch—kapow, baby!

HOW TO

1. Sift the flour into the mixing bowl and add the brown sugar, cinnamon, ginger, cloves, salt, and baking soda.

2. With two forks, or an electric mixer fitted with the paddle attachment, add the butter and mix until it forms the consistency of wet sand.

3. In a separate bowl, combine the molasses, rum, and egg.

SUPPLIES

(Makes 3 dozen men)

COOKIES

3¼ cups all-purpose flour

¾ cup firmly packed brown sugar

1 tablespoon ground cinnamon

1 tablespoon ground ginger

½ teaspoon ground cloves

½ teaspoon salt

1 teaspoon baking soda

12 tablespoons salted butter, cut into small chunks

¾ cup dark molasses

2 tablespoons rum

1 egg

ICING

½ cup confectioners' sugar

2 tablespoons water

SUGGESTED EMBELLISHMENTS

Toy car for roadkill marks (look for something with thick tread!)

Licorice ropes

Sugar cubes

Rock candy

Cocktail swords

4. Slowly incorporate the wet mixture into the dry. The dough will be fairly sticky.

5. Divide the dough in half and put each half on its own piece of waxed paper, lay a second sheet of waxed paper on top, and flatten slightly with a rolling pin until the dough is about 2 inches thick.

6. The dough will need to rest. You can freeze it for about 20 minutes, or refrigerate it for a couple of hours. The dough will keep for several days chilled, if you'd like to do these steps in advance.

7. Preheat the oven to 350°F. Generously grease two baking sheets.

8. Lay the chilled dough on a well-floured work surface. Roll flat until the dough is between $\frac{1}{8}$ and $\frac{1}{4}$ inch thick.

9. Cut out your doughboys and place them on the baking sheets about 2 inches apart. (Note: To make convincing tire tracks on a cookie body, you'll want to run the little man down before baking him.) Bake for 6 to 8 minutes, or until the cookies are slightly darker around the edges. Remove from the oven and leave on the baking sheet for 2 minutes before transferring to a wire rack to cool.

10. To make the icing, add the water to the confectioners' sugar a few drops at a time, whisking until it forms the consistency of thick toothpaste.

11. When the cookies have cooled completely, apply the icing with a pastry bag (or a resealable plastic bag with one corner snipped off) and embellish to your fiendish delight.

Embellishments

Few things give me more pleasure than embellishing a miniature crime scene. Small toys raided "from a kid's room" is a great place to outsource accessories. Whenever possible I like to make my vignettes edible. Licorice ropes and rock candy "ice cubes" appeal to my inner cannibal.

Here are some tips:
-- As well as being decorative, the icing works as a great glue for holding down red hot candy buttons and tiny weapons.
-- To make a "Frozen in Ice" gingerbread man, frost one cookie entirely and add a layer of clear and blue rock candies. Stack more icing and candy on top of one another until you've reached your desired thickness.
-- I like to serve these cookies on a giant piece of parchment paper set on my dining room table. I trace a body outline around each cookie, and as my guests eat away at the evidence, we're left with a macabre tableau of the gingerbread massacre that recently occurred. Bon appétit, indeed!

Dishes Best Served Cold

I love to have friends over for Mystery Dinner parties. Playing an amateur sleuth is always a refreshing juxtaposition of my usual modus operandi. My menus tend to reflect the party theme whenever possible, and the following is a list of some of my favorite dishes:

-- Finger Sandwiches
-- Red Herring on Toast
-- Tongue Salad
-- Liver with Fava Beans and a nice Chianti
-- Saturday Night Special
-- Smashed Potatoes on the Lamb

Flaming Amy: The Cocktail

Like any self-respecting evil genius, I have a nemesis. My frenemy isn't an agent for good, attempting to balance my evil creative transgressions with her own works of righteousness. No, my pal Amy is a craft stalker, plain and simple. If I make something unique and lovely, I'll see her the next day whipping up some facsimile, a Chinatown knockoff of my designer original. To call her a copycat, though, is a cheap shot; her cunning and quick draw with the pinking shears make her a worthy adversary.

In this misguided rivalry, she's found new lows—stealing my man, unleashing wild squirrels into my apartment, and jamming up my glue gun. She crossed a line when she shrank my favorite sweater. My fury screamed for vengeance.

Torching her accordion would be a clear violation of my parole conditions. A little stealth voodoo was in order, and what a treat it was to see little beef jerky effigies of my rival go up in flames, washed back in a tasty rum-drenched cocktail. And if my mojo is working, Amy should be feeling a bit hot under the collar right about now.

SUPPLIES

(Serves many)

SEASONING MIX

½ pound kosher salt

1 tablespoon ground chili

1 tablespoon ground coriander

1 tablespoon paprika

1 tablespoon lemon pepper

½ tablespoon ground celery seeds

Small resealable plastic bag

Small plate

Scissors

Beef jerky (see Note)

Thick, cheap, glass martini glasses

Tomato or veggie juice blend

Peppers, celery, or jalapeños for garnish

Rum--and it's got to be at least 100 proof. Today is really a 151 kind of day.

Matches

HOW TO

1. Place the seasoning ingredients in a small resealable plastic bag, and shake well. Pour onto a plate slightly larger than the rim of your martini glass. Set aside.

2. For each glass, use scissors to cut a small person shape from the jerky. Nibble on the scraps if you're feeling a bit peckish.

3. Press the rim of the martini glass into a damp towel, or dip it in a small bowl of water and shake off the excess. Because you'll be setting things on fire, make sure to use thick, cheap glasses for this one, and not Mom's heirloom crystal.

4. Press the rim of each glass into the seasoning mix.

5. Fill the glass three-quarters full with tomato juice or veggie blend. I go with V8--it has that breakfast feel.

6. Add your garnish--peppers, celery, and jalapeños are all nice accompaniments--and the jerk person.

7. Pour one liberal shot of 151 rum on top of the jerk person in each glass and let the person float on top of the glass or lean jauntily against the side.

8. Light the jerk with a match.

9. Bask in the glow, enjoy the moment, blow out the fire, *then* drink. *Don't drink this while it is on fire*--you *will* hurt yourself. Ouch!

Note:

Look for wide, flat pieces of beef jerky. Around 2 x 3 inches is ideal for a good voodoo doll. You can use turkey jerky for this, too. (It's fun to say and just as effective.)

Instant Disguise Drink Bling

Hardened cons, amateur spies, and parents of small children know the critical importance of carrying at least one change of clothing. It's embarrassing the number of times I've been caught out without a wig or fedora to hide underneath. Since I prefer to do my surveillance and crafting from bars, it's essential to have an accessory that can play double agent, such as a quick mustache/sunglasses disguise that doubles as a sassy glass garnish.

Making this craft item is about as easy as ordering a round of drinks. Enlarge the template and cut it out. Color in the design, or print on fancy papers if you want to outfit your whole crew. Tape a tall straw to the back of your disguise, and grab another drink—it's time to lie low.

SUPPLIES

Heavyweight printing paper
Crayons or colored pencils
Glitter (optional)
Straws
Tape

HOW TO

1. Copy the templates from the book. Experiment with sizes a bit; sometimes a teeny-tiny mustache is more fun than a great big one. I used a heavy printing paper, but fancy scrapbook paper would really make these disguises pop.

2. Color, glitter, or embellish the disguise, if you like. It makes a fun
    party craft, and is a great way for folks to figure out whose drink is
    whose.

3. Tape the disguise to a drinking straw and work on your cover story--
    you're now in hiding!

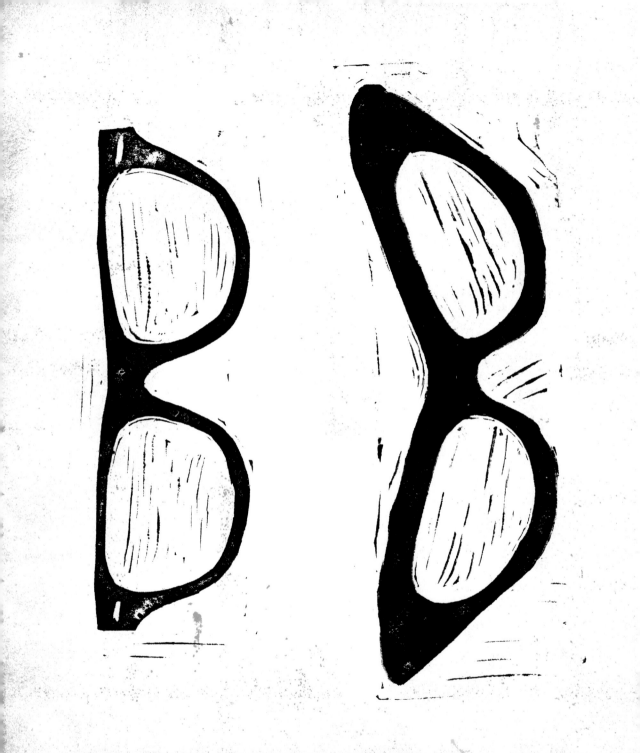

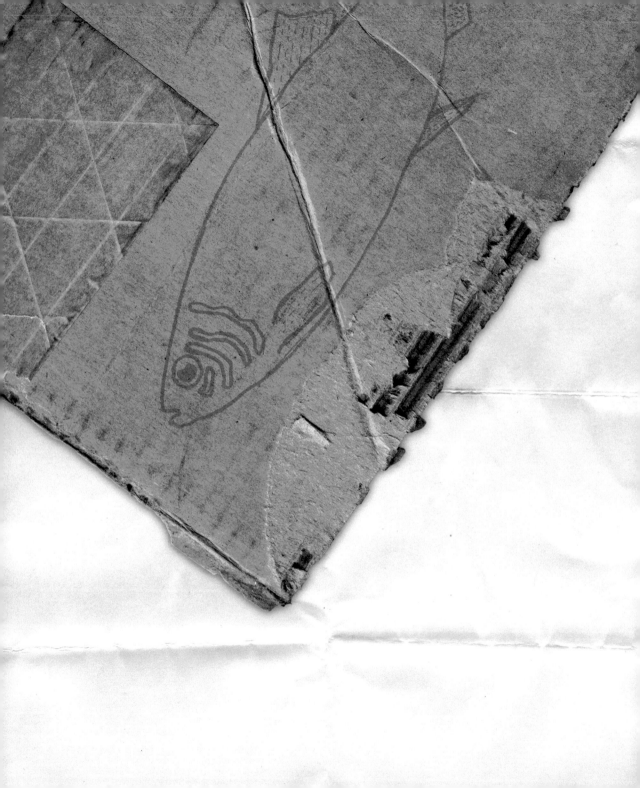

HOME IS WHERE THE ♡ HEART IS . . . AND THE LEFT LEG, AND THE SPLEEN

Decor for Your Den of Thieves

RED HERRING PILLOW

Tonight you sleep with the fishes!

Or maybe you don't. This felt softie is a slippery devil, a charmingly misleading enigma.

The pattern, when enlarged to 500 percent, makes an oversize herring—the perfect bedside body pillow, wooing heavy-lidded detectives into an uneasy slumber as they grasp for a solution to the crime, just out of reach, maybe somewhere in their gauzy dreams. As their attention is diverted, you slip out the back, Jack.

SUPPLIES

Scissors

Straight pins

Red polar fleece

Black felt for fins

Small scrap of white felt for eyes

Embroidery needle

Black and white embroidery floss

Red sewing thread

Sewing machine (optional)

Polyfill or other favorite stuffing

HOW TO

1. Enlarge the template 500 percent or to your desired size, then cut out the pattern pieces.

2. Pin the main body pattern pieces to the red fleece, then cut out.

3. Pin the fin and gill pattern pieces to the black felt and the eyes to the white felt, then cut out the pieces.

4. Using the black embroidery floss, sew a black iris on top of each white eye piece.

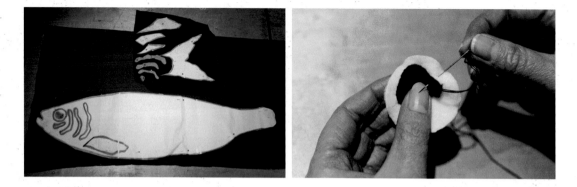

5. In long running stitches, embroider white stripes on all the fin pieces.

6. Appliqué the gills and eyes to both sides of the fish body.

7. Appliqué the pectoral fins to the fish body at the vertical seam.

8. Appliqué the tail fins on top of the fish's body at the seam mark.

9. Lay the fish sections right sides down. Using red thread, attach the pelvic, anal, and dorsal fins to the insides of the fish at the seam lines.

10. Pin the body pieces together with the right sides facing.

11. Stitch the body together, using a $\frac{1}{2}$-inch seam allowance and leaving a gap in the head area for stuffing. This step could be done by hand using a backstitch, but it will go much faster with a sewing machine.

12. Turn your fish right side out and stuff it with polyfill or your favorite stuffing.

13. Turn in the seam allowance at the stuffing gap and stitch the gap closed.

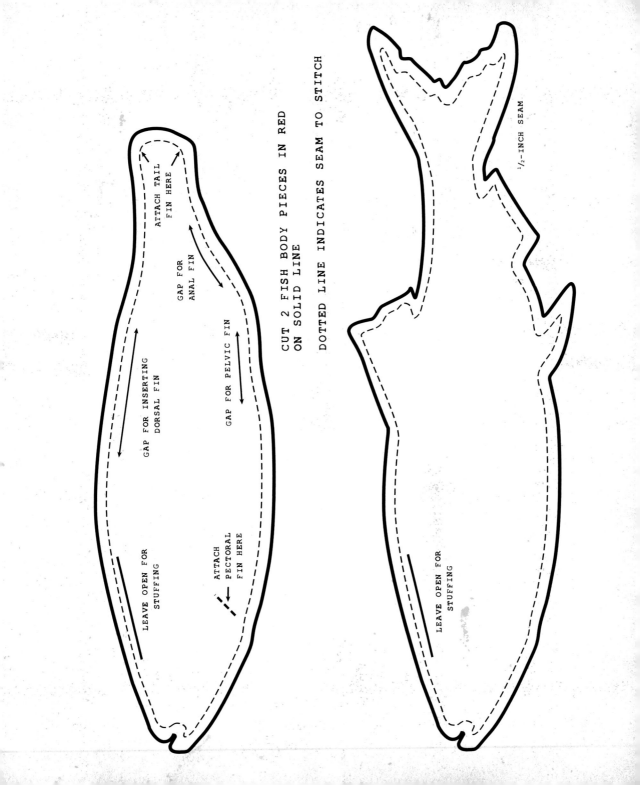

CUT 2 FISH BODY PIECES IN RED
ON SOLID LINE

DOTTED LINE INDICATES SEAM TO STITCH

ATTACH TAIL
FIN HERE

GAP FOR
ANAL FIN

GAP FOR INSERTING
DORSAL FIN

GAP FOR PELVIC FIN

LEAVE OPEN FOR
STUFFING

ATTACH
PECTORAL
FIN HERE

½-INCH SEAM

LEAVE OPEN FOR
STUFFING

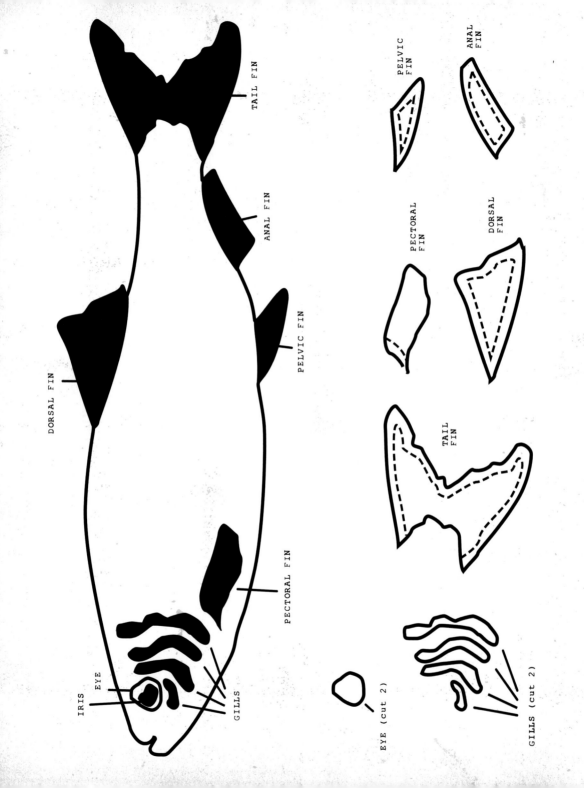

TAIL FIN

ANAL FIN

PELVIC FIN

DORSAL FIN

PECTORAL FIN

IRIS

EYE

GILLS

PELVIC FIN

ANAL FIN

PECTORAL FIN

DORSAL FIN

TAIL FIN

EYE (cut 2)

GILLS (cut 2)

Treasure Island, a Mystery Novel

With guest appearances in numerous movies and mystery stories, decoy books are the quintessential criminal craft and are a prerequisite accessory for a well-stocked den of thieves. Of course, I have several of the sly stashes and like to cut my pages into silhouettes of the objects hidden inside. Thank goodness encyclopedia sets are cheap these days, or I'd never know where to keep my flask collection.

Award yourself extra style points for finding books with ironic titles for your treasures—and for goodness sake, don't hide anything in your grandma's Bible, or *Crime and Punishment*; it's the first place the feds are going to look. This is experience talking . . .

SUPPLIES

Hardcover book

Large paper clip or clothespin

Small bowl

2 tablespoons craft glue

6 tablespoons water

Small paintbrush

X-Acto knife

HOW TO

1. Open the book, turn the first few pages toward the front cover, and fasten them temporarily in place with a large paper clip or clothespin. Leave the book propped open in this position while completing this craft. Leaving a few pages in the front of the book to move freely acts as a further decoy for your deception when the project is complete.

mount, a... such a... in the company of him as a...
ing... his... to think of him as...
...know... Pell

fal... to do? Re...
...ory that V...
it. ...looking on a li...
...e confusion a li...
...ase disconnec...
I set up my...
Blackwater R...
came down to excava...
building) whic... he Lax...
house) ... Blackwater...
pathway... a thou...
of this arc...
the bend... vict...
lichen-gr...
I had... ...wail op—Lax...
momen... in...
eigh...
"Ver... Seab...
...to have broug...
ai... in the Seabrokes...
...doubt about it," said I. "Laxton begin...
connection between Pell and the convict.

...er ascend to
...e, raised
...almost
...ously
...l was
...oan horse
...over the
...wplace Abbey
...the old guest-
...jecting over the
...re in the form
...of woods on
color of the
...door in the
...the door a
...him say,
...ning at
...f re... when
...und," said
...ll and the
Laxton can't
Seabrokes in...
his knowledge,
Do you get that?"
...lked

2. In a small bowl, mix the glue and water.

3. Paint the glue mix onto the outside edges of the book pages. You'll want the mix to lightly saturate the edges. Brush out any drips. Prop the book open to dry with the clipped pages at the front.

4. If you've got glue left over, cover your bowl with plastic wrap until you're ready for Step 7.

5. Reduce or enlarge the keyhole-shaped template so it fits onto the page of your book with a $\frac{1}{2}$-inch margin on all sides.

6. After the exterior pages are dry, trace the keyhole-shaped template onto the open book, again leaving a few loose pages in the front. Make sure the template is centered at least $\frac{1}{2}$ inch from the edge of the page before cutting.

7. With an X-Acto knife, cut the template shape into the book pages. If you press hard, you can usually cut two or three pages at a time. Take out the scraps and continue cutting until you've a nice, deep cavity for your treasures.

8. Paint the glue mixture onto the inside of the cavity. Keep the book propped open while it dries overnight.

9. Fill the compartment with your treasure and hide the book in plain sight. Don't worry, your secret is safe!

Barefoot Bandit Grass-Head Cellmate

Feeling lonely? Need a little buddy for company? My last trip to solitary was a bit like that. I found myself talking to the walls, the little voices in my head . . . Rather than fight the inner demons, I decided to make myself a real friend . . .

Amazingly, my pal Stinky was fabricated almost entirely from things I had with me in the pokey—an old sock, buttons from my work suit, dirt from the exercise yard. I had to trade my dessert cups for a month for the needle and thread, and the groundsman took my last pack of smokes in exchange for the grass seed, but my cool buddy was all worth it.

A former carny and grifter who just can't fly straight, Stinky is waiting for water, a little love, and a sunny window in which to grow.

SUPPLIES

Buttons for eyes

Old, unloved sock

Needle and embroidery floss for the eyes and face

¼ cup grass seed (see Note)

Potting soil or loose dirt

Rubber band

Coffee mug or similar container

Accessories (hair ribbon and eye patches are great)

HOW TO

1. Sew on the button eyes just beneath the toe seam of the sock, and use a running stitch to embroider facial features.

2. Pour the grass seed into the sock.

3. Stuff the sock with dirt, firmly packing it in. You'll want to put your hand inside the sock while doing this, making sure the dirt pushes the grass seed to the top and back of your grass buddy's head. Of course, if your buddy starts to sprout weird facial hair in the front, you can either pluck or trim it--that is half the fun!

4. When your sock is full, bind off the opening with a rubber band.

5. Submerge your pal in a bowl of water or run him under running water, letting the dirt become completely saturated.

6. Prop up your buddy in an empty coffee mug or other container in a sunny window. Spritz him every few days if he starts to dry out, or put him back under the faucet.

7. As your buddy's hair grows, trim and pluck as you see fit. Add the accessories of your choice.

Note:

I made Stinky from fast-growing wheatgrass, but really any variety will do. A lawn mix makes soft, fuzzy hair, and I've even done a feline treat of cat grass for the strays that live out back.

He'll last 6 to 9 weeks before becoming a bit moldy around the edges. At that point I'll probably compost my pal, perhaps harvesting his eyes for a replacement friend, Stinky II.

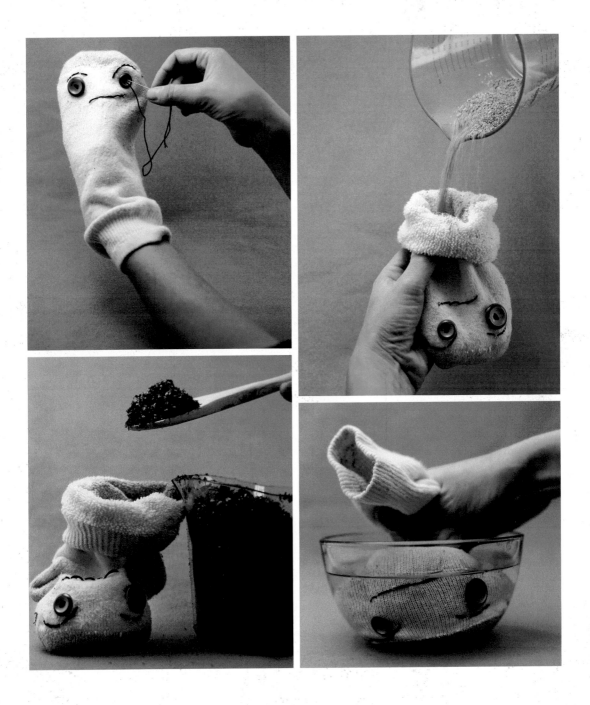

Board Game Throw Pillows

Arranging things is one of my favorite hobbies: funerals, bank jobs, occasionally flowers when I'm feeling ironic. Lately I've taken to messing with the furniture. The piano and the sofa are a bit of a challenge, but I've made sort of a game of hiding smaller objects, such as the candlestick in the drawing room, and the lead pipe in the kitchen.

My dinner guests (well, all but one) find this hilarious. The other afternoon our high jinks turned a bit tragic, when a loaded revolver was left in the conservatory. We're still trying to figure out who perpetrated that little crime! In the meantime, the Professor suggested I whip up these delightful pillows as decorative tokens of our after-dinner sport. It seems a bit safer, and infinitely more comfortable than a mislaid dagger in the drawing room—or in the ribs, for that matter.

The stencils for these pillows were made from freezer paper. It's an easy method for putting cool images on fabric, similar to silk-screening but without the equipment. A number of amazing craft bloggers have put tutorials up online, including Dana Made It (www.dana-made-it.com) and Portland's fabulous Angry Chicken (angrychicken.typepad.com). My thanks to them for the inspiration.

SUPPLIES

Scissors

Freezer paper (see Notes)

X-Acto knife

Iron

2 (18-inch) fabric panels per pillow (see Notes)

Old newspaper

Fabric paint

1-inch-wide paintbrush

Straight pins

Sewing machine, or needle and thread

Polyfill or your favorite stuffing

Fabric protector, such as Scotchgard (optional; see Notes)

HOW TO

1. Enlarge the template pattern to your desired size to fit on a finished pillow measurement of 17 inches square, and cut it out. My rope, revolver, and wrench measured about 12 inches.

2. Trace the stencil template onto a 16-inch square of freezer paper.

3. Use an X-Acto knife to cut the stencil from the freezer paper. Put your stencil, slick side down, on top of your fabric.

4. Set your iron at the highest nonsteam setting to ensure that the paper will stick completely to the fabric. Iron the stencil onto your fabric, starting with the large outline first, then pressing down any smaller pieces. It's helpful to initially press the iron onto the paper, rather than moving the iron around; this will tack the design down in place and keep the paper from tearing.

5. Lay out an old newspaper to protect your work space and put the panel to be painted on top of the newspaper.

6. Fill in the open area of the stencil with fabric paint. You'll probably want to do two coats for a sharp design, and wait at least an hour between each coat.

7. Let the paint dry overnight.

8. Peel the freezer paper off the fabric.

9. Pin the fabric pieces with right sides together.

10. Sew the pillowcase on all four sides with a $\frac{1}{2}$-inch seam allowance, leaving a 4-inch gap along one side for stuffing.

11. Flip the pillowcase right side out and stuff the pillow.

12. Hand-stitch the gap closed.

13. Assemble your guests in the drawing room and begin your interrogations.

Notes:

I used an all-cotton fabric, but you could use a poly blend as well.

You can find freezer paper at most grocery stores. This wrapping parchment has a paper side and a slick side that is coated in a light wax.

I covered my pillows in a fabric protector when the project was finished, as, you may have surmised, my conservatory does get a bit "stain happy."

Concrete Slippers Window Shade

Is there a spy in the house of love? Rather than telling the nosy neighbors and Peeping Toms to take a long walk off a short pier, craft up a clever privacy screen that artfully gets your veiled threat across while letting sunlight in and keeping your secrets safe. In this quiet undersea crime wave, an ever-so-subtle, cement-booted silhouette contemplates a peaceful repose as he sleeps with the fishes. Could there be a more perfect watery imagery for your bathroom window?

SUPPLIES

Scissors

Removable vinyl adhesive paper

Masking or painter's tape

Newspaper or tracing paper

Spray frost

HOW TO

1. Enlarge the template to your desired size for your window and cut it out.

2. Use a pencil to trace the design onto the vinyl adhesive paper backing and cut it out.

3. Temporarily tape the paper templates to your window to determine final placement.

4. To create a water line at the top of your window, draw on newspaper or tracing paper a wavy pattern that is 4 at least inches deep and the width of your window. Cut out and tape the paper water line onto the top of the window.

5. Peel the vinyl fish and mystery man stickers off their backing and apply them to the window.

6. Follow the manufacturer's directions to coat the windows with spray frost. To get a crisp image, you'll want to use at least two coats.

7. When the frost is completely dry, peel the stickers and the wavy pattern from the window. After your hard work of crafting and scheming, you've earned a bath. Recline back in the tub and contemplate how lovely hot water can be when you get into it willingly and how pleasant it is when you can keep your head above it.

CRiME SceNe CARPet

J ohnny Law popped 'round the other afternoon for an unexpected visit, and, boy, was my living room in a state—lamps and tables turned over, dishes broken, magazines torn, glitter and craft supplies strewn about the place. Most embarrassing was the unidentified, unexplained corpse sprawled on the floor. It really was every hostess's nightmare, especially as I'd run out of sherry. A very tedious afternoon followed, with endless questions and lab assistants taking hair samples and photographs. Despite the chaos, I couldn't help but admire the flashy police accessories, and I began to covet their skills at interior decorating.

I was especially fond of the chalk outline on my carpet, the bold black-and-white graphics a subtle contrast to my paisley drapes. Chalk has the tendency to smudge and fade, however, so I decided to find a more permanent and memorable embellishment for my favorite hearth rug.

SUPPLIES

Roll of inexpensive gift-wrapping paper for making the stencil

Masking tape

A willing victim (see Notes)

Marker

Scissors

Solid-color rug (see Notes)

1 can white spray paint

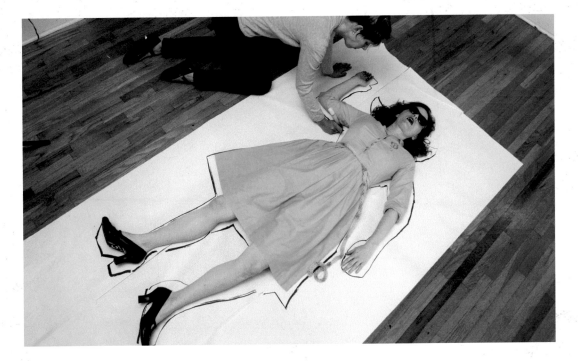

HOW TO

1. Tape out two or three long sheets of cheap wrapping paper side by side for the victim to pose on. You'll want lots of extra paper around him or her--at least 12 inches--to leave room for the outside portions of the stencil.

2. Use a marker to trace the outline of your principal character. Staging this is important--splayed legs and gesticulating arms look best.

3. Remove the victim, then trace a second outline about 2 inches outside the first, all around the entire body.

4. Carefully cut the inner and outer stencils from the paper, discarding the 2-inch strip of paper in between the two drawings. This will be the area where you apply the spray paint.

5. Take your carpet outside or to a well-ventilated place, and don't try this on a windy day--your paint won't spray evenly and the stencils could get blown off the carpet.

6. Tape the inner stencil to the carpet from behind, in your desired position.

7. Again taping from behind, attach the outer stencil to the carpet.

8. Apply several coats of paint to the exposed carpet space, waiting an hour between each coat.

9. Your rug memorial is ready to go. You can walk and tramp across it to your heart's delight, and the design is fine to vacuum over.

Notes:

I was able to pick up a shag carpet at a major-brand hardware store for under $50. As it's now the centerpiece for my living room, it was a pretty thrifty investment.

Because you'll need to manipulate the body and move it around a few times, I'd suggest using a live model. While it may be easier to trace a body after rigor mortis has set in, it tends to be fairly heavy and harder to reset into poses.

Midnight in the Garden of Good and Evil

Sometimes it's the little things in life that give us the greatest pleasure, like kicking back and watching Mother Nature's passion play. Ferocious battles to the death can take place in our very living rooms. Like Nero Wolfe, I've taken a morbid interest in horticulture and have developed a particular fondness for mean plants—the kind you have to watch your step around.

Carnivorous Venus flytraps and pitcher plants are freaky-looking and devious, preferring to feast on live flesh. They like a hot, muggy environment—like a Carolina springtime—so, to keep the little monsters happy, I've built them a fancy-pants terrarium complete with headstones to honor the little fly soldiers that just couldn't compete in the Darwinian crapshoot.

SUPPLIES

¼ cup uncooked alphabet pasta

Small glass or metal bowl

2 to 3 tablespoons calligrapher's ink

Oven-bake polymer clay, such as Fimo or Sculpey

Toothpicks

Craft glue

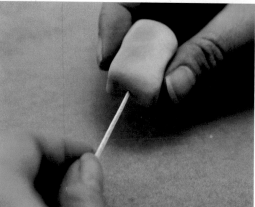

HOW TO

1. Pour the alphabet pasta into a small glass or metal bowl. Add the ink and stir until thoroughly coated. Add more ink if needed.

2. Lay out the letters on several layers of paper towels to dry.

3. Shape the clay into small headstone shapes of your desired size.

4. Insert toothpicks into the bases of the headstones, with 1 inch protruding from the bottoms.

5. Bake the headstones according to the clay manufacturer's instructions. (Remove from the oven and let them cool completely.)

6. Glue the dried letters to the fronts.

7. Stick the completed headstones into the ground.

8. Mourn.

Sources

John Dillinger Soap Gun

MELT-AND-POUR SOAPS, FRAGRANCES,
AND COLORANTS
Bramble Berry
2138 Humboldt St.
Bellingham, WA 98225
Toll-Free: 877-627-7883
Telephone: 360-734-8278
www.brambleberry.com

GUN-SHAPED CANDY MOLD
Sugarcraft, Inc.
3665 Dixie Highway (Ohio Highway 4)
Hamilton, OH 45015
http://www.sugarcraft.com/

Día de los Muertos Bath Fizzies

CALAVERA MOLDS
Reign Trading Company
3838 Walnut Grove Ave.
Rosemead, CA 91770
Telephone: 626-307-7755
E-mail: reigntrading@earthlink.net
www.mexicansugarskulls.com

FIZZY MIX AND SOAP SUPPLIES
Bramble Berry
2138 Humboldt St.
Bellingham, WA 98225
Toll-Free: 877-627-7883
Telephone: 360-734-8278
www.brambleberry.com

Grace Kelly's Rear Window Shades

MIRROR PAPER
JoAnn Fabric and Craft Stores
www.joann.com

RETRO SUNGLASSES
Naked City Clothing
3730 SE Hawthorne Blvd.
Portland, OR 97214

Pulp Fiction Pendant

GLOSSY ACCENTS, PENDANT BASE, AND
NECKLACE CHAIN AND CLASP
Collage
1639 NE Alberta St.
Portland, OR 97211
Telephone: 503-249-2190
www.collagepdx.com

Hell in a Handbag

MAGNETIC TAPE
JoAnn Fabric and Craft Stores
www.joann.com

Glue Gun Bandolier

SEAT BELT WEBBING, BELT BUCKLE, AND
METAL SLIDE HOLDER
Jax Outdoor Gear
1200 N. College Ave.
Fort Collins, CO 80524
Toll-Free: 800-987-9059
Telephone: 970-221-0544
E-mail: storemanager01@
jaxmercantile.com
www.jaxmercantile.com

Crime Scene Tape Messenger Bag

OFFICIAL CRIME SCENE TAPE
Crime Scene
3440 N. 16th St., Suite #4
Phoenix, AZ 85016
Telephone: 623-565-8573
Fax: 602-274-7280
www.crimescene.com

Martha's No-Knit Prison Poncho

If you want the real deal, rather
than having to make one yourself,
Xiomara Hernandez, the designer
who hand-crocheted Martha
Stewart's gorgeous "Coming Home
Poncho," will custom-make one for
you, too . . .
www.xiomaracreations.com

Mom's Cake with a File Inside

DECORATIVE BAKING SUPPLIES
The Decorette Shop
5338 SE Foster Rd.
Portland, OR 97206
Toll-Free: 800-728-CAKE
Telephone: 503-774-3760
Fax: 503-771-9718
E-mail: info@thedecoretteshop.com
www.thedecoretteshop.com

Absinthe Makes the Heart Grow Fonder

DECORATIVE WIRE
JoAnn Fabric and Craft Stores
www.joann.com

About the Author

With her glue gun registered as a lethal weapon at the local PD, Shawn Gascoyne-Bowman is one of the few women in America who has successfully placed a restraining order upon herself. She teaches workshops in social media for artists in Portland, Oregon, hosts an afternoon comic club, and is a martyr of a mother. She has ten years' professional cooking experience at the notable Colorado restaurants Q's, the Brown Palace, and Jimmy Schmidt's Rattlesnake Grill. In Germany, she worked as a pastry chef at the Dorint Hotel, and served breakfast to spies on behalf of the U.S. Army (no foolin'!). She dallied briefly in a promising East Coast film career, but decided to chuck it away to raise a demanding and ungrateful family and an ill-tempered dog. She worked for Martha Stewart for one day while living in New York. It didn't go well.

About the Photographers

These sinister siblings have spent a life on the run, mostly from wild animals such as bloodthirsty chipmunks and malicious mallard ducks. To stay under the radar, they pose as well-meaning educators of children, spreading laughter like a plague. Learn more at www.sisbro.com.